AN INSIDER'S GUIDE
TO SUB-MODALITIES

AN INSIDER'S GUIDE TO SUB-MODALITIES

Will MacDonald and Richard Bandler

*Sub-modalities are the fine distinctions
we make in each representational system:
the difference that makes a difference.*

Meta Publications Inc.
P. 0. Box 1910, Capitola, CA 95010
(408) 464-0254 Fax (408) 464-0517

Library of Congress Card Number 88-060928
I.S.B.N. 0-916990-22-2

TABLE OF CONTENTS

v

AUTHOR'S NOTE

All of the material included in this book is based on the work of Richard Bandler. Of Richard and his teaching, I am reminded of a passage from the *Tao te Ching:* "The sage does not hoard. Having bestowed all he has on others, he has yet more." (Translated by C.D. Lau, Penguin, 1969.) In preparing the text, I have drawn extensively on workshop transcripts in which Richard was teaching the concepts and practices of sub-modality usage.

Will MacDonald
Seattle

1 *Shades of Meaning*

What we are going to be experimenting with, within the broader frame of the structure of human subjective experience, are called submodalities. Modalities are the representational systems: visual, auditory, kinesthetic, olfactory and gustatory. We take information in from the external world using our five senses, and those same five senses are used internally to process information. We see pictures, hear sounds and have feelings on the inside.

When Neuro-Linguistic Programming (NLP) first began to study subjective experience, the structure of meaning was found to occur in the specific sequence of representational systems a person used to process information. These representational system sequences were called strategies. (See *NLP VOLUME I* for a detailed discussion of representational systems and strategies.) Later it was discovered that the intensity of meaning held a direct relationship to the sub-modalities, or the component elements, of a given representational system. For instance, as you remember a pleasant experience, the degree of pleasure you have in that memory is a direct consequence of the color, size, brightness and distance of the visual image you hold in your mind's eye.

People use predicates (verbs, adverbs and adjectives) specific to the representational system they are functioning in. They will say things like, "She just tunes me out" or "I don't see any alternative" or "I'm trying to come to grips with the problem." Indeed, as you listen to the language people use, they are much more specific than that. You must begin to hear the language they use to describe their experience and to take it literally. People will talk about "needing to get things in perspective" or "wanting some distance" from a problem. (See TABLE 1, page 43 for a list of predicates that describe sub-modality distinctions.) These sub-modality descriptions will tell you more about what is influencing someone than if you make the grosser distinction of making pictures or having feelings.

To discover how sub-modalities function, the first step is to learn that they do indeed exist. The best way to do this is in small increments, slowly and methodically. Practice this with someone else; then you can learn to do it with yourself, and it is important to be able to do it with yourself. The practice with another person is a kind of dissociation that makes the learning easier.

NLP is not a set of techniques; it is a methodology. Re-framing, for instance, is not NLP; re-framing is a byproduct of NLP. NLP makes models and re-framing is just one of the models. The methodology of NLP requires you to go slowly and to make comparisons. Concentrate on the methodology in the exercises. Specific techniques will come later, but first the methodology, which is the process of discovery from which specific techniques were derived.

The first piece of NLP methodology is to find out if the person you are working with did what you asked. How many times when you have asked someone to go inside have they gone in and done the wrong thing because they either jumped to conclusions or your instructions were inexact? When you are directing your own brain or when you are changing someone else's, you have to get rid of as much metaphorical description as possible. Brains are literal. To operate on this level means that you go down to the most basic components of brain processing. From what we know at this point, those basic components are the sub-modalities. In this exercise, you will begin to notice that it takes a very small incremental shift in the structure of subjectivity to be able to make a change. Beginning to do this slowly and methodically is also the process by which you will sort out the sub-modalities and begin to understand how to make transitions in your own brain.

EXERCISE: EXPLORING VISUAL AND
        AUDITORY SUB-MODALITIES

Group of two. One of you is Person A and the other Person B.

Step 1. *Person A identifies a past, very pleasant event. Do not share the content, and since you are* not sharing content you can pick an experience that is really juicy.

Step 2. As Person A remembers the event, Person B (using the sub-modalities list, TABLE 2, page 46) instructs him to change the sub-modalities of that memory one at a time. Remind him to put the sub-modality back to its original configuration before going on to the next change.

Step 3. Person A changes the sub-modalities of the memory slowly. Discover which sub-modality changes affect the memory the most and which affect it the least: affect it by making it more pleasant or less pleasant. Notice, as you go through the changes, if a change in a single sub-modality results in spontaneous changes in others both within the same system and across systems. These are called 'critical sub-modalities' and they will have the most impact on the memory.

Person B takes careful notes for Person A.

Step 4. Change roles and continue with Person B as subject.

Step 5. Change roles again, and Person A picks out an unpleasant experience to remember. Select something you would define as mildly unpleasant, something that was annoying or frustrating. This is not the place to experiment with major trauma.

Repeat the sequence of sub-modality shifts as before and compare the two memories. Do the same sub-modality shifts intensify/diminish both memories, or is there a difference?

Step 6. Change roles and continue with Person B as subject.

Take a break and then repeat the exercise using auditory sub-modalities. For the present, stay with those two. We will deal with kinesthetic sub-modalities later on. Now it is useful to have the kinesthetic as a check. After each change you can ask, "Is it more pleasant or less pleasant?"

For most people in most circumstances, as the brightness of an image is increased, the intensity of their responses increases. Likewise, for most people in most situations, as the volume of internal sound is increased (as it gets louder), the intensity of their feelings increases. Of course, there are contextual variations. If you remember a romantic, candlelight dinner, turning up the brightness will begin to diminish the romance. If you remember being locked in the cellar, where it was dark and scary, turning up the brightness will diminish the fear. What is important is that for any given experience, there is a difference that makes a difference—a sub-modality adjustment that results in a different response.

Most people do not use their brains deliberately; that is, their responses are automatic. Have you ever noticed that when you had a bad experience some time in your life, not only did you get to have it once, you got to have it over and over again inside your head? Let's say you had an argument; you walk away and find yourself still arguing. Three hours later and you are still in the same argument all by yourself. You go to a movie and see a film like JAWS or PSYCHO or THE EXORCIST. After you leave the theater and go home, you see the horror of it all as much as when you were in the theater. Or you re-live a past memory and it is just like being there.

Another example of an automatic response is when people criticize themselves inside their heads and feel bad. This is the "critical parent" of Transactional Analysis. Who is criticizing whom? Who's in there? To change the response, to use your brain deliberately, is not so hard. Listen to the voice and notice the tonality, the pitch, the rhythm. Also notice how you feel when you speak to yourself in that way. Now, remember someone who said things to you that you liked in a particularly delightful way. Hear that voice inside your head. Then change the content and say those critical things to yourself, the ones that made you feel bad, in that pleasant and delightful tonality. Notice how differently you are able to respond to the same critical words.

There are a number of implications to the idea that all behavior is the consequence of learned responses. The response to a given stimulus may be automatic, but as a learned response, you can learn something different: you can learn to respond in a way that is more useful. I worked with a woman who heard a voice urging her to kill herself. She had been listening to this voice for twenty years, and although she had never acted on its urgings, the voice terrified her and she was afraid that one day she would act. When I asked her to listen to the voice and decide how it was she knew to take the voice seriously, she said that it was the way the voice sounded that was impelling. She had been trying to get it to stop saying those things for the past twenty years without success. However, she was able, very quickly, to change the way in which it said them. She could speed the voice up, with an accompanying rise in pitch, until it sounded like a chipmunk in one of the cartoons. She could slow it down until it became unintelligible. She could make it sound like Donald Duck. The whole thing became ludicrous and she was able to laugh at it. Then, even though she was able to hear the voice in its original tonality, it no longer affected her the same way. Once she discovered she could control the process, her response was no longer automatic.

Once, when my daughter was three years old, I heard a terrified scream coming from her bedroom. I went charging in to see what was wrong and found Jessica sitting on her bed screaming that there was a monster in her room. When I couldn't find it, she said that I had frightened it when I came into the room and it was hiding under the bed. We got down on our hands and knees and looked. She assured me that this was her very own monster. I said that since it was her monster and she had created it she could make it any size she wanted. She could make it bigger. That was too frightening. She could also make it smaller. That pleased her and she shrank it down to a comfortable teddy bear size. That night we went out for dinner, and nothing would do but that Jessica take her now-friendly monster with her. On the way home, there was a wail from the back seat and Jessica was tearfully explaining that she had forgotten her monster in the restaurant. Her brother, a sophisticated six, said, "That's all right, Jess; I have him in my pocket."

If behavior is the consequence of a learned response, then change requires that something else be learned in its place. It is not enough simply to learn something new. What is implied here is that whatever is to be learned, if it is capable of producing change, must utilize the same mechanism as the old pattern. As an example of this, pick a recurrent memory, one you think about a lot, one that makes you feel bad. See what you saw and hear what you heard at the time. Memories do not involve seeing yourself in the event except in experiences like an automobile accident, in which a person automatically dissociates as a protective mechanism to diminish the horror of the event. Be certain that this memory does make you feel bad. Knowing that it makes you feel bad, run the memory forward all the way to the end, then run it backward. Take a few minutes to think about the experience and discover whether or not it still makes you feel the way you did. Reversing the order of an experience is one way to change the impact of an unpleasant memory. The mechanism is the same but is utilized in a different way by resequencing the parts of the event.

Phobics are people who have learned to be terrified of something. For a person who is phobic of elevators, he cannot not be terrified the moment he steps into an elevator. There is a structure to the phobic response, and this person cannot not access the particular meaning elevators have for him. A phobic is so terrified he cannot imagine himself having an experience with the thing about which he is phobic. He could not do what you have just done (reversing a memory) if it involves his phobia. Consider someone who was involved in a drowning accident and has a phobia of water as a consequence of that accident. For him to remember the incident in explicit detail, seeing and hearing exactly the same event, is terrifying. The experience and the memory of it are overwhelming. The question is, if the memory of the experience is overwhelming, how can you utilize the mechanism of the phobia to initiate change?

The first thing to do, in dealing with a phobia, is to shift the time frame. When a phobic thinks of the experience that generated his phobia, he is in a place of danger; however, he can back up his memory to before the event took place, to a time when he was safe. Also, however terrible the experience was, he did survive and he can go forward in time past the event until he is again in a place of safety. This places the traumatic event within a larger frame of experience. In memory, he will be moving from a safe place, through the event, to another safe place. By itself, the contextual shift is not enough to allow the person to go through the memory. It is only the first step in the process.

The next step is to have the person dissociate from the memory. That is to see himself at that other time and place. Seeing yourself in an event has a different emotional impact than a true memory. To prove this to yourself, remember a time when you rode on a roller coaster. See what you saw and hear what you heard as you sat there in the car while the roller coaster went up, up, up, over the top and down the big dip. Stop the movement and step outside of yourself so that you see yourself sitting there. Start the movement again and watch yourself sitting in the car as it goes down the big dip. Feels different, didn't it? This dissociation can allow the phobic to approach the memory of a traumatic event in a relatively non-threatening way.

To make the memory of the experience more comfortable, the person can project the images on the wall, getting a little distance from them. This makes it a two-part dissociation. To make it a three-part dissociation, the person can also see himself in the present as if he were in a movie theater looking from the perspective of the projection booth. He can see himself sitting there watching himself on the screen at that other time and place where the event happened. It is a good idea to anchor this three-part dissociation so that if the person begins to associate in the event you can fire the anchor and hold him out of it.

Begin by having the person see a still picture in which he sees himself in safety before the event took place. Let that picture go and have him see himself in a second still, again in safety, after the event is over and he knows he survived. That gives him a beginning and an end for the memory. Go back to the first still, before the event. Be sure that image has been projected on the wall. Have the person then see himself in the present, sitting with you and watching himself at that other time and place. Set your anchor for the three-part dissociation and have the person add movement to the image. Have him go all the way through the memory to the second safe place and then stop the movement. Bring him back into his body and then associate with that second safe picture, seeing what he saw and hearing what he heard after the event was over. Have him run the sequence in reverse—fast. It's as if he put the projector in reverse, all the way back to the first still picture. Associated in this way it should be a full VAKO (visual, auditory, kinesthetic, olfactory/gustatory) experience, except that it is going backward. This utilizes the mechanism of the old pattern and it will eliminate the phobic response.

An immediate behavioral test is useful to assist people to change what they believe about themselves. If someone has been phobic for twenty years, it is difficult for him to believe he can change so quickly. I worked with a woman who was claustrophobic, who could not go into a telephone booth and close the door. After we ran the phobia cure pattern, I suggested she go to a phone booth and call two friends who knew she had a fear of closed spaces and tell them what she was doing. She came back glowing and talking about how marvelous she felt telling her friends she was in a phone booth with the door closed. This was a nice opportunity to make a lot of jokes about how difficult it will be to get her to come out of those small, closed places. Each joke takes her back through the new pattern and serves to reinforce it.

If a behavioral test is not appropriate or available at the time, you can begin to talk about the thing about which she was phobic and notice her responses. Then future pace. Ask her to think of something that hasn't happened yet, but might, that in the past would have produced a phobic response. Have her play through that imagined event as if it were happening to her and notice her response. This is something she could not have done with the old phobic pattern intact. Another approach to the future pace is to ask, "If this pattern works, what would you be able to do that you could not have done before?" Once she has identified that behavior, have her imagine doing it and enjoying the activity. It is one thing to be able to do something, but to experience pleasure in the activity that was terrifying represents a much higher level of change.

Fun and laughter are important ingredients in any change work you do. In fact, if you don't have a sense of humor, you cannot do NLP: it is one of the requirements. I worked with a nine-year-old boy who had a phobia of snakes. He was playing in the barn, picked up a handful of hay and found himself holding a snake. His response to the incident was extreme and he had not slept through a single night in the ten months following the incident. The first thing I did was to ask him where he thought the snake was now. I answered my own question: "Probably hiding down in his hole. When his Mommy asks him why he doesn't go to the barn to play, he tells her about the boy who picked him up and yelled at him and threw him around." He thought this was really funny and we laughed about how silly the snake was. Then I told him the story about Jessica and her monster.

Going into the event from the point of view of the snake gave him a new perspective. We joked about who was more frightened, him or the snake. If the snake could make that kind of mistake, so could he. Jessica's story introduced the idea that he could control the process that was terrifying him, and certainly if a three-year-old could do it, a big nine-year-old like him could, too. The stories and the laughing made it easier to do the rest of the work, and he was able to go home and sleep all night by himself without dreaming about snakes.

If, as sometimes happens, a person cannot remember the original experience, the one that produced the phobia, have him identify three different experiences in which he had a phobic response, three different contexts in which he was phobic about the same thing. Change the first, the earliest, using the same technique you would use with the original experience. Then change the other two in the same way. These patterns generalize and will result in a change in the phobic response.

Phobias themselves will generalize to other experiences. I worked with a woman who was phobic of bridges where you could see through the grating to the water below. After making a change in an experience with a bridge, she said, "No, it's the sound of the tires on the bridge that triggers the fear." We then worked with the sound, which produced nausea. Changing the response to the sound led her back to the sounds of a boat motor in a high sea. She had been in a storm as a child, was lashed in her bunk, seasick, vomiting, water washing over the deck, hearing her father say they were not going to make it, and as a background to the whole experience she heard the sound of the motor straining in a following sea. Once that was changed, the total pattern was freed and there was no longer a response to bridges.

You should have some sense by now of the utilization of the mechanism of the old pattern to teach something that will replace that unwanted pattern. So let us take that principle and begin to apply it in a way that will affect your patterns in a way that is useful. In this exercise you will be doing something that is very simple. There are processes you understand, so you recognize the sensation of understanding. You have also been confused at times, so you know what it feels like to be confused by something. Most people, when they are confused by something, go about gathering more information on the subject. That tends to confuse them even more. The difficulty is not that they don't have enough information but that they do not have the information organized in a way that is useful. This exercise deals specifically with the organization of information.

EXERCISE: CONFUSION TO UNDERSTANDING

Pick a partner and designate one of you as Person A and the other as Person B.

Step 1. *Person A will identify something he understands and something he is confused about. You must distinguish between confusion and ignorance. When you do not have any information, or very little, about a subject, you are ignorant about it. You are confused when you do have information, but have not yet figured out how to use it.*

To avoid confounding this experience with the training, do not pick anything that has to do with the content of Neuro-Linguistic Programming.

Step 2. *Person B is to find out the following: when Person A thinks about what he says he understands, does it have certain sub-modality characteristics? Also discover if or how those characteristics are different when he thinks about something he does not understand or is confused about.*

Do not ask what it is he understands or is confused about. Here is an example of the procedure.

B. Do you have something you understand and something else you are confused about?

A. Yes.

B. Do they both have pictures?

A. Yes.

B. Are they both movies, is there movement in them, or are they still pictures—like a slide?

A. Understanding is a movie, but confusion is like a bunch of slides one after the other.

B. Do they both have sound?

A. Yeah. In understanding, there is a voice telling me what to do. When I'm confused, I hear myself saying, "I don't know" over and over again.

Use the old trial-and-error method. Go through the sub-modalities list from TABLE *2, page 46, and find out the difference in your partner's internal representation of the state of understanding and the state of confusion. Each time you find a difference, write it down on a piece of paper.*

Step 3. *When you have finished eliciting the sub-modalities of understanding and confusion, have your partner change confusion to understanding by adjusting the sub-modalities of confusion to match the sub-modalities of understanding. In the example quoted, a typical dialogue would be as follows:*

B. When you think about the thing you are confused about you have a series of still pictures. Fill in between them with more pictures until you have enough pictures there to make a movie.

Are you still confused?

A. Yeah.

B. Listen to the pitch, the tonality, the rhythm of the voice you hear in understanding. Now change the voice that was saying, "I don't understand" until it matches the voice of understanding.

Are you still confused?

A. Sort of, but the voice in confusion is beginning to describe the pictures I'm seeing.

Continue down the list of differences you made until the person is no longer confused, changing the sub-modalities of confusion in to the sub-modalities of understanding one at a time.

Step 4. *Change roles so that you each have the opportunity to elicit sub-modalities and experience change by adjusting one sub-modality configuration into another.*

The following is a transcript of Richard Bandler working with the sub-modalities of confusion and understanding to provide additional insight into the process.

R.B.   What did you discover? You have no excuse now. Anything you are confused about... make it make sense. People discover in this exercise that they know more than they thought they knew.

N.   I found in the confused state that there's an internal volume that is real loud and that keeps me from hearing and seeing and everything.

R.B.   (Shouting) What?

N.   When you turn the volume down I become...

R.B.   Oh, okay. If you have a loud noise in your head, it would make it hard to...

N.   To hear and feel.

R.B.   Like having children... not being able to hear yourself think. Well, if you had a very loud... was the volume your very own internal voice?

N.   I didn't check out whose voice it was.

R.B.   Hopefully it was yours. Or maybe it was your parts.

P.   Volume is the one I used because that's the one she kept repeating over and over again. She had no picture in the confused state, but when she turned the volume down, she got a picture. It got clearer. It became like the one in understanding.

R.B.   What's your name?

N.   Nicky.

R.B.   When you did that, Nicky, did you have the experience of understanding? When you did what he is describing?

N.   No. What I had was more options. I didn't feel so stuck.

R.B.   Okay, but did you change it so that it was the same as understanding?

N.   I felt that it would... it would move me to more understanding.

R.B.   I'm hoping that. I just wanted to go all the way.

N.   That's the sense I have, is that it would go somewhere.

R.B.   Why don't you change it the rest of the way and find out?

N.   I don't know how to do that.

R.B.   Once you changed it, was there any difference where you got the understanding? When you understand, did you have a brighter picture, more pictures, was one a movie and the other slides?

N. There was more awareness of all sounds around.

R.B. No. Is there a difference between when you are in a state of understanding and a state where there is more movement? Probably in that state you would get some understanding eventually. I'm just trying to find out if there was a difference between when you understand and when you're in a state of movement. A state of movement may be better—problem with understanding is you could be wrong.

Learning to manipulate the sub-modalities (like color, focus, size, distance movement, pitch, volume, location) is the first step in developing the flexibility to control your internal states. This is new and it does take some practice. These are phenomena that, for the most part, are out of conscious awareness. They are, however, processes of which you can become aware. The way to do it is to stop, go back to the beginning of a memory and go through the event again. Slow down in order to find out what the structure is. As you remember a particular event, do you first see a picture in your mind's eye and then hear voices? What are the visual and auditory sub-modalities? What is the sequence in which you do things? Most people have a tendency to make this more complicated than it really is. The difficulty is learning where to look for simplicity. Sort of the elusive obvious.

There are common problems associated with learning to deal with sub-modalities. Some people will say that they cannot make pictures. Others are good at making pictures, but do not know how to change the volume of the sounds they hear in their heads. Some are good at making pictures, but cannot control them; changing size or distance, for example. There is the person who says he cannot listen to something and hear it again inside his head. But this is a person who can hear his mother's voice saying, "You're just like your father." He is simply not making a choice, not using the mechanism deliberately. The capacity to control these processes deliberately, so that you can participate in the response (at least now and then) is worth having.

The Richard Bandler transcript continues:

R.B.   How about the rest of you? Did you find out what happened as you began to take the structure of confusion and change it in to understanding? What happened?

G.   It produced an understanding for me. Several things changed... like the size of things.

R.B.   Put them in proportion, so to speak.

G.   Another was changing from still pictures in the confused state to slide into a motion picture.

R.B.   There is a lot more information there.

G.   Definitely. Gets you moving.

R.B.   You take those slides and turn them into a moving picture and it gets you moving. Makes sense.

A.   The opposite was true for me.

R.B.   That makes sense.

A.   If I took the picture where I was having confusion, that picture was moving. The picture in which I was understanding was a series of stills. I didn't see myself actually moving. I can make it move, but it distracts me.

R.B.   It distracts you?

A.   Because there's all this stuff going on all of a sudden.

R.B.   That's the difference. Now, what is going to be interesting is that you are going to try somebody else's process of going from confusion to understanding.

A.   He'd not be a good person for me to try.

R.B.   Ohhh, quite the contrary...

S.   Before we go on, I have a question about something I did. My partner had a picture for one situation but not really for the other. She had feelings for the first one and not for the second. There seemed to be no auditory channel for either, so I had her install an auditory channel for both. That was the only way I could get a channel that was shared by both experiences.

R.B.   We weren't trying to share a channel for both experiences. We were just trying to change one into the other.

S.   But if you've got a picture for one and not for the other...

R.B.   Then you make a picture of it—just straight ahead.

S.   I wasn't able to get a picture to stabilize.

R.B.   Where did the picture come from in the first place? How did she know what to make a picture of?

S.   The picture was just there.

R.B.   *A priori*? Now, you have to understand that when people report to you, they are telling you the best they know. That's when you have to start backing up. In this instance, you have to ask her how she knows what to put in the picture. Let's say you had to try her confusion. You had to be confused about something the same way she was. She had feelings when she was confused or when she understood?

S.   When she was confused.

R.B.   If you are going to try her confusion, how do you know which feelings to have? She had to select what she was confused about and then have the feelings. How did she choose?

S.   She had many, many pictures.

R.B.   That's when she was confused?

S.   Right. I couldn't get them to stabilize.

R.B.   (To L) There have been things that you didn't understand and then you did?

L.   Right.

R.B.   How did you... is the clear picture a still or a movie?

L.   It's a still.

R.B.   How do you go from having many, many pictures to getting a still?

L.   I don't know.

R.B.   Can you think about something you used to be confused about? Is it just one still or is there a series of stills?

L.   Oh, it could be a series of stills. I was thinking of this particular thing I understood. It was just a still picture.

R.B.   And is it in focus?

L.   Yes.

R.B.   She can get a picture in focus and stabilized; she just doesn't know which one. Now, out of the thing you were confused about, can you take another picture and put it in focus?

L.   Okay.

R.B.   Now, do another one. Another. And another. And they all have that "not quite right" feeling.

L.   Yeah.

R.B.   Now, close your eyes for a minute and look at all five of them. Now squish them together. Watch what happens. Just as if you put a hand on either side and pushed them into one picture.

L.   I think I did it.

R.B.   Keep watching it. Now, straighten it out. Make it clear. Do you have a single slide now?

L.   I think so. I don't know what it's of. I feel different, but I don't know that I see any particular picture now.

R.B.   You have to tell us. Do you have one clear slide? If it's not clear make it clear. Quit wasting our time.

L.   How did I get myself into this?

R.B.   You paid money. Think about that. You were probably confused at the time.

L.   I still am.

R.B.   There is another way to approach this. That is just one way. I was just demonstrating for people. It's not important. The other thing you can do is go back and take one of the clear slides and notice when it doesn't feel quite right. Like some of your feelings don't match it. Take just those feelings and adjust what is in the slide until you get that part to feel right. And just change what's in it. Part of it at a time, by adjusting... in other words, doesn't quite feel right... make an adjustment until you get part of your feelings to change. And then maybe another part. And another part. Try that.

The process of making the transition from confusion to understanding in this way enables you to gain practice in eliciting and shifting sub-modality patterns. As you become more adept, you will also gain an understanding of how sub-modalities function in subjective experience.

What you are dealing with is the structure of experience, as opposed to the content of that experience.

"Confusion to understanding" is a misnomer in a sense. Making the transition from confusion to understanding is something we all do in the activity of learning. The difference is that in the past you have not made the accompanying sub-modality shifts deliberately. The next step would be to utilize another way of organizing information, another way of learning. This will provide you with a greater degree of flexibility. The way to do that is to use someone else's way of going from a state of confusion to a state of understanding.

EXERCISE: USING ANOTHER PERSON'S PROCESS

Work with the same partner you had in the last exercise.

Step 1. *Person A identifies something he understands. You can use the same content as in the previous exercise, or select something different.*

Step 2. *Person B, using the notes from the previous exercise, will instruct Person A in changing the sub-modalities of his understanding into Person B's confusion.*

Step 3. *When Person A has become confused in the same way that Person B is confused, then Person B will instruct him in making the sub-modality changes to Person B's way of understanding.*

Step 4. *Change roles and repeat steps 1 – 3.*

What happens when you use someone else's process of going from a state of confusion to a state of understanding is that you use his method of learning, of organizing information. Choose carefully when doing this and select someone whose strategy is efficient and effective. When you want to learn something, find someone who learned it quickly and easily, then do it his way, using his system of organizing information. When you attempt to learn things in a way that does not work then you stay confused or worse, incompetent. When you learn in a way that does work, confusion gives way to understanding in a predictable and therefore repeatable process.

What does all of this say about content? It says that the content was already there. In other words, you were capable of understanding with the information you already had. Sometimes people do not have enough information to enable them to reach a state of understanding, but when they go through this process of organizing information by sub-modality shifts they discover the missing pieces. They will then know precisely what information they need in order to understand. This is not a vehicle to prevent you from feeling confused; it is a vehicle by which you can know more—a lot more. Of the things you already know, your brain is capable of knowing even more. All you have to do is structure the information so that it is organized differently.

Every experience you have, whatever you call it (confusion, understanding, motivation, excitement, etc.) has a structure. The purpose of these exercises is to give you more understanding of that structure. What you have been discovering is that the representational systems are gross distinctions and that we represent our experience with much finer distinctions, which are the sub-modalities. The sub-modalities are also systemic in that they tend to affect one another. Did you, for instance, notice a change in the auditory portion of your experience as you brightened your picture?

There are relationships that exist in nature, relationships our brains have learned and applied to internal processes. When something moves off into the distance, the volume of sound generated by it decreases. Think of a pleasant experience, seeing what you saw and hearing what you heard at the time. Move that image off in the distance and notice if the sound diminishes. As a way of generalizing, think of the relationships in nature, but as with everything else in NLP check your assumptions before acting on them. In particular, listen carefully to the language people use to describe their experience. As a way of exploring your own processes, you can reverse some of the spontaneous patterns you use. For instance, if an image gets smaller as you move it into the distance, begin to make it larger as you move it away from you. What happens to the sound when you do that? How does that alter the way you feel about that experience?

A lot of what we are going to go through here together will enable you to create techniques that are far better than any you have learned. You have integrated NLP into thinking when you are able to listen to somebody and can make up an effective technique there and then, easily. This is more useful than to remember reframing, for example, and apply it as a formula. All this requires is that you know how to use your brain deliberately and that you have a few examples to work from.

This next piece, once again, involves the elicitation of sub-modalities. There are things you want to do and the doing of them is easy and natural—that is called being motivated. Then there are other things you want to do and somehow you do not do them—you lack motivation. The process of motivating yourself to do something has a structure, just as there was a structure to your gaining understanding. You are going to begin by searching through your experience to find an example of something you were highly motivated to do, and did. You will also find an example of something you wanted to do and were not motivated and as a consequence did not do it.

Watching yourself in a dull, fuzzy picture may produce a feeling of being stuck, but if you associate (looking at the scene as if you were there) the whole picture may change and produce an entirely different feeling. That is a piece of useful information. Sometimes we find ourselves motivated to do things we do not want to do. In that case, dissociate and look at yourself doing whatever it is you don't want to do as a dull, fuzzy picture. It is not as appealing that way and might just keep you out of a lot of trouble. Sometimes context has an influence on which sub-modalities make a difference. For instance, slowing the movement in one context may be necessary to motivate you, while in another context it will be necessary to speed up the movement to get you in the flow. For some people who need to get a grip on things, it may be necessary to stop the movement altogether for them to motivate themselves.

As you explore someone's motivation strategy, it will be easier for him to respond accurately if you give him a choice by asking questions that offer a comparison. For instance, "Is it in black and white or in color?" "Are you associated or do you see yourself in the picture?" You will also want to pay particular attention to the sequence in which they do things because it is the sequence that moves them from one state to another. Again, use the trial-and-error method and go slowly. If you were to simply ask them, "What do you do inside your head when you motivate yourself?" they will probably say something like, "Well, I think about it and then I get this feeling." The sub-modality distinctions you are exploring here are not conscious, for the most part, but they are distinctions a person can become conscious of. It is the conscious awareness of the process that gives us the possibility of change.

The following is a transcript from a workshop in which Richard is teaching motivation strategy elicitation.

TRANSCRIPT

RICHARD: How do you get yourself up in the morning? When you wake up you have to motivate yourself to get out of bed. You don't just find yourself standing on the floor. How do you do it?

WOMAN: When I'm still asleep a little voice wakes me up.

RICHARD: Goes, HELLO.

WOMAN: It does different things. The other day it was saying, "You didn't set your alarm for the right time. If you wait for the alarm, you will be an hour late so you better get up."

RICHARD: So, it wakes you up by making you feel bad. That's a nice way to start the day. IF YOU DON'T GET UP YOU'RE GOING TO BE LATE. And then you don't feel so comfortable in bed anymore. Create enough discomfort and she'll want to get out of bed because it's no fun to be there. A lot of people do that. If they say something and it's not quite bad enough then they have to say something worse. One threat after another until it's too annoying to be in bed. There's the old bladder technique. Brain goes, "So you don't want to get up, take this." But how do you do it?

WOMAN: What motivates me?

RICHARD: We just went through this. How do you motivate yourself? Do you make a picture of yourself doing it and then step inside the picture and find yourself doing it?

WOMAN: What motivates me to bang out of bed in the morning is so I can have a cup of coffee and a cigarette before the kids get up and motivate me to go crazy for the day.

RICHARD: When you're lying in bed, do you see yourself smoking a cigarette and drinking coffee, make the image brighter and then step into it?

WOMAN: I don't know. I, ahhh...

RICHARD: This may happen in a second for you. That's because you have learned to do it very well. There's no reason to interrupt it. But you can still, if you stop and go back, just go back in your head. Close your eyes and you hear your alarm. What happens?

WOMAN: Another day.

RICHARD: So you say, "Another day." Then what? Just go back and listen to the alarm. Listen to what you say.

WOMAN: I just don't know. I just...

RICHARD: Okay. The way to find out is you go back. You listen to the alarm and just keep running through it. Find out what happens. If it goes by too fast, go back to the beginning, feel yourself totally relaxed and hear the alarm. Being able to take the time to find out that things can go by too fast for you is important. The faster it goes the more it takes to slow it down enough to find out what happens.

MAN: I know what I tell myself if I wake up and then how I get out of bed. As far as waking up, it seems automatic. I say I want to get up at a quarter after seven in the morning and exactly at a quarter after seven my eyes open up. And I don't know how it works.

RICHARD: It works in hypnosis with everybody. We do have an internal clock that knows what time it is. What you do is you program yourself. Most people will say, "I have to get up at eight, or maybe eight-fifteen, and if I hurry I could sleep until eight-thirty." Then the brain goes, "Well, if you can't make up your mind, to hell with you. Buy an alarm clock." Whereas, you say, "I have to get up at seven-fifteen," and whoosh, it works. But if you don't say anything before you go to sleep...

MAN: Yeah, you have to say something. Say it specifically.

RICHARD: What if you didn't? What happens then?

MAN: Might never wake up.

RICHARD: Listen to what he said. He said, "You HAVE to say something specifically." If you pay attention to the language people use, they will tell you what is going on.

MAN: For me, the important thing was the beginning and the end of the visual pictures.

RICHARD: The importance was the beginning.

MAN: And the end. Otherwise it was running.

RICHARD: How did it keep running if you didn't have an end? How do you tell an end from a middle?

MAN: There wasn't any end to the pictures I was having.

RICHARD: So that's when you couldn't get motivated?

MAN: Right.

RICHARD: Whereas if you had a specific place to begin and a specific place to get to then you became motivated. I bet you can follow instructions well if they are good instructions.

MAN: Yeah.

RICHARD: What you are going to be doing is finding out what another person does to motivate himself. In other words, his motivation strategy. The rest of that, to know if you have indeed determined his strategy, is to pick a content and be able to have the person do what it is that you describe... does it motivate him? In other words, can you motivate him to do something that is fairly irrelevant? So, if I want to motivate him to pick up this pen. I say make a picture of me going like this (snaps fingers) as a beginning. And see yourself doing the thing or do you see what you would see if you were doing it? How does it work? What goes on in the middle?

MAN: It starts with a picture.

RICHARD: Is it a slide or a movie?

MAN: It starts as a slide and it starts moving.

RICHARD: You start with a slide. Then it's a movie. And then you end with a slide. Is that what it means to have a beginning and an end?

MAN: Oh.

RICHARD: Well, that makes sense. He's got both. That's clear. Now, the movie in the middle. Does it have sound?

MAN: Yes.

RICHARD: Is it you talking to yourself or hearing what would occur at the time?

MAN: Hearing activity.

RICHARD: Hearing activity. Do you see yourself doing the activity or do you see what you would see if you were doing the activity? Start with the slide, the first slide.

MAN: I don't see myself. I see what I'm doing.

RICHARD: So you would, for example, you would see the pen over here in the slide.

MAN: Yeah.

RICHARD: Then you would see your hand reaching out, grabbing a hold of the pen and picking it up. And that would then stop there as a slide. Okay. Go ahead and try it. It works.

MAN: Yeah.

RICHARD: See, if we hadn't started with a still or if he had seen from the outside of the movie... For example, let me have the pen back. Now, see yourself reach over and grab the pen. Doesn't get you off. Alright. Now go back and do it the other way.

MAN: Just like a robot.

RICHARD: Okay, try something. This time what I want you to do is to make the same images, the ones that made you go over and get the pen. Okay. Go ahead. Keep making them. You got a beginning, run it through to the end, only don't get the pen. Isn't that an eerie feeling in your hand? Okay. Now when you make it it doesn't motivate you now. You can see the pen over there. You can see the hand reaching out picking up the pen. Okay. Go ahead and do it. [Man picks up the pen.]

See, there was a piece missing. You don't ever want to leave a piece out. He's a man who can follow instructions. If I told him to just make the pictures, it's not enough. That just gives him something to do. There had to be the task, "Go ahead and do it." The human body functions in relationship to activity.

WOMAN: You lost me with that.

RICHARD: When I told him to just make the pictures of the activity, he saw the pen, he saw his hand moving towards the pen and he saw his hand picking up the pen, but I didn't tell him to do it. Which means inside the strategy there is an auditory component that tells him when to begin. He knew where to begin, but he didn't know when. He could just keep making the pictures of doing it, but there wasn't anything that said, "begin now." It wasn't like he was trying to resist or put it off. It's a funny feeling. He was waiting. It wasn't that he wanted to get the pen and couldn't. His hand was poised, ready to go when I said, "Go ahead and do it."

This exercise will give you the opportunity to elicit a motivation strategy and to confirm the accuracy of your elicitation.

EXERCISE: ELICITING A MOTIVATION STRATEGY

In pairs.

Step 1. *Person A selects something he was really motivated to do. Something he wanted to do and doing it was easy and natural. He then selects something else that he wanted to do but where he lacked the motivation and did not do it although he wanted to.*

Step 2. *Person B, using the sub-modality lists, will find the difference in those two experiences: motivation and lack of motivation. Pay particular attention to sequence; the strategy has a beginning, middle and end.*

Step 3. *When Person B thinks he has enough information to make the strategy work, pick some simple, irrelevant task and find out if you can motivate your partner to do it.*

Step 4. *Reverse roles and repeat steps 1 – 3.*

When you are eliciting a motivation strategy, you want to be sure the person picks something about which he was truly motivated. He should pick something that when he thinks about it he starts drooling out of the corner of his mouth and starts stomping on the ground. The strategy you elicit from that will be much more functional than if it were an 'oh hum' kind of experience. The point to the exercise is to get the other person to do something irrelevant as if it were the most natural thing in the world. If he has to push, if it does not work easily, then go back and find the piece that is missing.

Now that you know how to motivate yourself, you can begin to anticipate this next sub-modality elicitation. Have you ever really wanted something; and when you got it it was "sort of O.K.?" It is one of those times when looking forward to the event was more fun than the event itself. Disappointment requires adequate planning—requires foresight. You just cannot be randomly disappointed. Then there were other times when you went along with an experience, "just making the best of things." For some reason that has a negative connotation. Finally, there have been times when you were in such a good mood that no matter what happened, you had a better time than you should have had. We have all had experiences where we went into a situation and influenced it in such a way as to make it more pleasurable and more productive than anyone could have anticipated. Remember a time like that.

Somehow or other there are times when you get juiced. Those are the times when you know what a good time is—not just an "oh, I feel fine" time and not just an "Okay" time. Okay is not good enough. What is it that you do internally that gets you to be juicy and to have fun? Sometimes you feel you just cannot get there. Well, let's find out where the throttle is.

EXERCISE: MAKING THINGS BETTER THAN THEY SHOULD HAVE BEEN

In pairs with, where possible, a different partner.

Step 1. *Person A selects some experience where he "made the best of things." He then selects another experience where he made things better than could have been anticipated. There is a real difference in attitude between that and "just making the best of things."*

Step 2. *Person B elicits the sub-modalities of both experiences. When you think you know Person A's strategy for making things fun and exciting, stop.*

Step 3. *Person B will then take his partner through the strategy in which he will make the experience he is having now into an experience that is fun and exciting. Too many people have the activity of sitting still connected to learning. This is an opportunity to find out if you can change somebody's experience of the moment so that it is more enjoyable.*

Step 4. *Reverse roles and repeat steps 1 – 3.*

This exercise was designed to enable you to utilize the sub-modalities of a present situation in order to affect a person's ongoing experience. This can make the activity of participating in a workshop or study group more fun, livelier. However, life in going to go on and some of the more severe psychological problems like boredom and certainty are the new horizon of what we are going to have to learn to deal with.

Boredom and certainty are functions of behavioral constraint. There are times when you would like to be more competent or vivacious. If you were less conservative and took certain kinds of risks, you would be operating more as the kind of person you want to be. Those are situations where some feeling gets in your way, some feeling that impedes your ability to act in a way you would like. You think about taking a risk and the feeling stops you, but you do not know for sure whether it is a risk if you have never taken it.

Richard was in a seminar some years ago in which they had something called a trust circle. This is an exercise in which the group forms a circle around someone and the person on the inside leans over and everybody passes him around. When the person got to Richard, Richard jumped back and, "Blam," the person hit the floor. He jumped up and shouted at Richard, "Why did you do that?" Richard said, "Without risk, there is not trust."

The person who is trusting and taking the risk is the person on the outside who lets go. The one on the inside is just playing the game by the rules. The danger is not that great—the floor is not that far away. If you want to find out what it is to take a risk, break the rules. Most of the time you will discover it is not a matter of life and death. If you are looking for the limits of what you can do and what you are capable of, the best way to find those limits is to pretend you can do anything. What you cannot do, you won't. It is simple. Just because you try five times and fail does not mean you won't be able to do something eventually. If you worry about what you cannot do, the best way to find out is to go ahead and do it. What you cannot do, you won't. That is something you can feel secure in—takes the risk out of everything, so to speak.

It is all a matter of your point of view. So you go out and begin to do certain things because it all sounds so logical. You go out there and encounter whatever constitutes risk for you. You say, "What I cannot do, I won't and I'm gonna do it." Then there is a little monster inside you that reaches up and grabs a handful of your gut and your body goes into spasms. That is one of the kinds of feelings people have in lots of different situations. There are other feelings you get at times that I know you do not like. This exercise will enable you to change your feeling response to situations that in the past have limited you in some way.

EXERCISE: 'CHANGE HISTORY' WITH SUB-MODALITIES

In pairs. Person A as the subject.

Step 1. *Person A identifies some feeling he has that results in a limitation; a feeling that results in a constraint on his behavior and flexibility; a feeling he would like to change.*

Step 2. *Person B is going to help him find three different contexts, three totally different situations in which he had this feeling.*

The procedure is the same as in 'Change History' in which Person A thinks of a time when he had this bad feeling: seeing what he saw and hearing what he heard at the time. Person B anchors the feeling. Pattern interrupt and then Person B holds the anchor while A goes through his memory, B watches his face and when he sees strong examples of the feeling, he tells him to make a picture of the event that is occurring. The anchor will hold A's feelings constant while he sorts through his memories to find examples of situations in which the feeling is common. Age regression is allowed.

Step 3. *Once the events have been identified, find what sub-modalities are common to each of them. Until now, you have been comparing the sub-modalities in paired experiences (like confusion and understanding) to find out how they are different. In this exercise, you will find out which sub-modalities are the same in these experiences. The kinesthetics are from the same feeling response so the shared sub-modalities will most likely be visual and auditory.*

Step 4. *The sub-modalities that are common to each of these experiences are an intrinsic part of the feeling response. Person B will then assist A in changing those sub-modalities into the sub-modalities A discovered in the last exercise:* MAKING THINGS BETTER THAN THEY SHOULD HAVE BEEN.

Step 5. *Person A identifies a context, a situation that has not happened yet, but which might, that in the past would have resulted in his limiting feeling. Have him go through that situation, changing any sub-modalities that are common to the old feeling he does not want; changing them in to the sub-modalities of* MAKING THINGS BETTER. *Think of a few more contexts that have not happened yet, but which might. Find out what happens as you go through those in your imagination.*

Step 6. *Reverse roles.*

Following is a transcript of Richard working with a group that has just completed this exercise.

R.B. How did you do with this?

J. It seems like the visual component of the memory is one thing and the visual I was having at the time is another thing. So if...

R.B. That's true.

J. In remembering now... it's like it changed certain aspects of that experience. How does that have anything to do with when I had that experience at that time or I run into a similar situation? I mean, I blew up those memories. I can relate to that.

R.B. If you go back and think about... and see the same thing you saw at the time it occurred. How does that make you feel?

J. Yeah, it worked. I have a different...

R.B. Go back and see the same thing you would see if it were occurring now. Okay. Does that answer your question?

J. What that says to me is if I was in that situation, I would do something else now.

R.B. Close your eyes and construct one. Imagine a new one and find out. Imagine a situation that you would most likely predict would have those unpleasant feelings. Alright. And create it so it is a new one. Make it as real as you possibly can in your mind. Find out what happens.

J. Okay.

R.B. Nooowwww!

How about the rest of you? Any questions before we give it full throttle?

L.   I was sure that I helped my partner to have fun in the experience in the past that she was seeing, but I'm not at all sure that's going to happen when she is confronted with the actual situation again.

R.B.   Rushing ahead. We are going after the lasting ones next. The thing is, if you can change your perceptions about a memory, and then the big question is, when you get out in the real world, how do you get the same things to make you feel different? The sub-modalities you were changing were changing the feelings to make it feel fun. You see, the notion of risk can be looked at as an unprecedented opportunity. You know, you can call it risk or you can call it RISK. Those are two different attitudes. The first step was to make it something enticing.

The next chapter deals explicitly with the structure and sequencing of sub-modality changes to ensure that the changes you get will be lasting ones.

Table 1

SUB-MODALITY DESCRIPTIONS IN LANGUAGE PATTERNS

People tend to speak in predicate sets (verbs, adverbs and adjectives) that specify the representational systems they are attending to consciously and that provide information about the sub-modality distinctions they are making.

Listen carefully to the language people use and take it literally.

VISUAL

Things were blown out of proportion.

My job seems overwhelming.

Life is so drab.

I need some distance from it.

He's had a colorful past.

That throws a little more light on it.

It all seems so hazy.

I don't know, it just flashed on me.

When you said that I just saw red.

That brightens up my day.

Well, when you frame it that way, yes.

She has a sunny disposition.

That hits too close to home for comfort.

I need to bring things more into perspective.

It just appears flat and meaningless.

I'm glad we see eye to eye.

Everything keeps spinning around and I can't seem to focus on one thing.

It's too vague even to consider.

It's off in left field somewhere.

The image is etched in my memory.

I just can't see myself being able to do that.

He's got me up on a pedestal.

She cut him down to size.

I'm moving in the right direction.

I can't face it.

It's not a black and white world.

This is top priority.

Let's look at the big picture.

AUDITORY

The right decision was screaming at me.

She gives me too much static.

It's just a whisper.

If I nag myself long enough, I'll do it.

There is too much discord in our relationship.

I hate that whining part of myself.

Got you, loud and clear.

We need to orchestrate our vacation.

It came to a screeching halt.

I keep telling myself, "You can't do anything right."

It's too off-beat.

KINESTHETIC

It's got a slimy feel to it.

He's hot.

She's a cold fish.

Whenever I hear that, my stomach knots up.

The pressure is off.

The whole thing weighed on my mind.

I'm off center, like everything is out of kilter.

I'm trying to balance one against the other.

Yeah, I feel up to it.

NOTE: This is only a partial list of the sub-modality descriptions used in everyday speech. Consider it as a beginning and add to it as you become more aware of your own language patterns and those of the people you come in contact with.

Table 2

SUB-MODALITY DISTINCTIONS

VISUAL	SOME QUESTIONS TO ELICIT THE DISTINCTION
Color/black and white	Is it in color or black and white? Is it full color spectrum? Are the colors vivid or washed out?
Brightness	In that context, is it brighter or darker than normal?
Contrast	Is it high contrast (vivid) or washed out?
Focus	Is the image sharp in focus or is it fuzzy?
Texture	Is the image smooth or rough textured?
Detail	Are there foreground and background details? Do you see the details as part of a whole or do you have to shift focus to see them?
Size	How big is the picture? (ask for specific, estimated size, like 11″ × 14″)

Distance	How far away is the image? (again, ask for specific, estimated distance, like 6')
Shape	What shape is the picture: square, rectangular, round?
Border	Is there a border around it or do the edges fuzz out? Does the border have a color? How thick is the border?
Location	Where is the image located in space? Show me with both hands where you see the image(s).

Movement:

Within the image	Is it a movie or a still picture? How rapid is the movement: faster or slower than normal?
Of the image	Is the image stable? What direction does it move in? How fast is it moving?
Orientation	Is the picture tilted?
Associated/dissociated	Do you see yourself or do you see the event as if you were there?

Perspective	From what perspective do you see it? (If dissociated) Do you see yourself from the right or left, back or front?
Proportion	Are there people and things in the image in proportion to one another and to yourself or are some of them larger or smaller than life?
Dimension	Is it flat or is it three-dimensional? Does the picture wrap around you?
Singular/plural	Is there one image or more than one? Do you see them one after the other or at the same time?

AUDITORY

| Location | Do you hear it from the inside or from the outside? Where does the sound (voice) originate? |
| Pitch | Is it high-pitched or low-pitched? Is the pitch higher or lower than normal? |

Tonality	What is the tonality: nasal, full and rich, thin, grating?
Melody	Is it a monotone or is there a melodic range?
Inflection	Which parts are accentuated?
Volume	How loud is it?
Tempo	Is it fast or slow?
Rhythm	Does it have a beat or a cadence?
Duration	Is it continuous or intermittent?
Mono/stereo	Do you hear it on one side, both sides, or is the sound all around you?

KINESTHETIC

Quality	How would you describe the body sensation: tingling, warm, cold, relaxed, tense, knotted, diffused?
Intensity	How strong is the sensation?
Location	Where do you feel it in your body?
Movement	Is there movement in the sensation? Is the movement continuous or does it come in waves?

Direction	Where does the sensation start? How does it get from the place of origin to the place where you are most aware of it?
Speed	Is it a slow steady progression or does it move in a rush?
Duration	Is it continuous or intermittent?

2 *Inherent in the Movement*

What we have been doing so far is a contrastive analysis of the sub-modalities of two states, like confusion and understanding. Then we have changed the sub-modalities of one into the other without paying attention to the way of making the change or the sequence of sub-modalities being changed. However haphazard the process, changes did occur. The question now is, how can the sub-modality shifts be utilized to make permanent change?

Memory patterns provide a clue to how long-term behaviors become established. Take an experience that, as we remember it, we would describe as overwhelming, and the image with which we remember this overwhelming experience is very large and very close. Somehow we have learned to remember the experience with this particular configuration of sub-modalities. There are other sub-modality characteristics to consider as well as size and distance, but for the sake of simplicity we can concentrate on these two. The intensity of the experience and the number of times we ran the sequence of internal images during the event were factors in teaching our brains how to recall that event.

Consider the experience of a little girl being chased by her older brother who is holding a garter snake and yelling, "I'm gonna get you." During this experience, she is focused on a limited number of things: her brother's face, the snake in his hand, the sound of his voice and the feeling of the snake on her back. She is concentrated on that awful snake and sees it both externally and in her mind's eye. The projected feeling of the snake inside her dress intensifies the images. The sequence is rapidly external/internal, because she also has to watch where she is running. Since her focus is limited, the internal image expands to fill her whole field of view. This is a process she may repeat a hundred times in her wild dash around the garden. This is a learning experience, and each repetition reinforces the pattern until now, as an adult, any encounter with a snake reproduces that internal image and the feelings that go with it. The brain does not distinguish between feelings you like and feelings you do not like. It has simply learned to associate certain feelings with certain experiences.

Adding information, "The snake is harmless and cannot hurt you," is not sufficient to break the association of snakes and her feelings. Size and distance were important in the original event, and every time she sees a snake there is an internal image that gets bigger and closer. The process can result in feelings that are so intense that cogent recollection of the event is lost.

You will remember in the phobia cure the person sees herself go through the event. Changing the point of view so that she sees herself prevents the narrow focus (snake getting bigger and closer) and enables her to maintain a broad perspective. Restructuring an entire event in this manner sometimes provides people with information that was blocked from consciousness.

A Vietnam veteran had a recurrent memory in which he sees the body of a dead child lying in a rice paddy and knows that he killed him. When he went through the event in dissociated images, seeing himself at that other time and place, he was able to watch his squad enter the village, he then saw four figures running out of a hut and across the rice paddy, he saw himself open fire, then he watched himself walk to where the bodies lay and turn one over. It was the body of the child, but with a new perspective on the event he realized that at the time he fired he did not know it was a child. Associated, with the image of the dead child filling his entire field of view, his feelings were so intense that the event itself was blotted out of memory.

The sub-modality distinctions made here and in the case of the girl with the snake are analog distinctions. Before we explore the possibilities of using them to make permanent change, it is necessary to understand the difference between analog and digital sub-modality distinctions. Analog distinctions can be changed slowly or quickly along a continuum. For example, the image of the snake can be made larger or smaller in one smooth transition. Digital distinctions are those that are mutually exclusive: if you are experiencing one you cannot experience the other at the same time. Association and dissociation are digital distinctions. Either you see yourself in a memory or you remember the event by seeing what you saw at the time. You may shift back and forth very rapidly, but not both at the same time. An analogy can be made with a light switch. Digital distinctions are like an on/off switch—light is either on or off. Analog distinctions are like a rheostat—light goes from off to on in a smooth progression as quickly as you turn the knob.

As you work with people, pay particular attention to the critical sub-modalities, those that affect other sub-modalities both within the same system and between systems. For some people, distance will affect size, brightness and color. As they move an image farther away, it also gets smaller, dimmer and less colorful. It may also shift them from being associated to dissociated. As they continue to move the image farther away, at some point they pop out of the image and become dissociated. Distance may also affect volume and tonality in the auditory system. Even small incremental changes in a critical sub-modality can have a profound effect on your experience because so many other things change with it.

This next exercise is a chaining sequence in which anchors will be used to induce movement in the sub-modalities. As an example, think of a pleasant experience. Then begin to brighten the image and continue to brighten it slowly until you find the optimum brightness, that is, the degree of brightness that feels most pleasant. Anchor the memory at that point. In the process of determining the optimum brightness, you may go too far and the memory may begin to feel different. Stop and dim it down again until you find the brightness level that is most pleasant. An interesting area for speculation is how we code memories and whether pleasant memories are coded differently from unpleasant ones. Now think of the pleasant memory again as you did in the beginning, fire the anchor and notice what happens to the image. Does it get brighter? What happens to your feelings during the time of brightening?

EXERCISE: ANCHOR CHAINING ENHANCED WITH SUB-MODALITIES

In pairs.

Step 1. *Person A identifies a feeling that stops him from engaging in a behavior that would be fun but that he considers to be slightly outrageous. Whatever that would be, he only thinks it would be outrageous because he has never tried it. As he imagines doing it, it looks outrageous. It is the kind of thing he thinks would be fun, but says to himself, "I could never do that."*

Step 2. *Find at least two analog distinctions (critical sub-modalities) that vary simultaneously to diminish the feeling that stops him from engaging in the behavior he has identified as 'outrageous.'*

The sub-modalities are not used to change the feeling, only to diminish it.

Step 3. *Person B has A diminish the feeling and anchors the feeling in its diminished state. That is anchor #1.*

You are going to use three anchors in this exercise. One way to make it simple is to use the knuckles on one hand of the person you are working with. These anchors can be discrete and are easily available for chaining.

Step 4. *Person A then identifies a resource he would need in order to engage in the 'outrageous' behavior. This does not mean he will rush out to begin acting outrageously. This exercise is about creating possibilities. The behavior will appear more attractive, perhaps even becoming a possibility in appropriate circumstances.*

Step 5. *Person A remembers a time when he had access to that resource: seeing what he saw and hearing what he heard at the time. B anchors the resource state. That is anchor #2.*

Step 6. *Find the critical sub-modalities that will intensify the feelings of the resource state. Have A intensify those feelings and anchor them with anchor #3.*

Step 7. *Test the anchors and calibrate to the external manifestations of the internal states. Be sure that each anchor is discrete and that the feelings are strong. If there are any questions, check with Person A and if necessary, go back and re-set one or more anchors.*

Step 8. *To establish the chain, fire anchor #1; just before the internal state peaks, fire anchor #2 and release anchor #1. Test by again firing anchor #1. Notice if there is a transition to the resource state of anchor #2. If not, check your work at this point and repeat whatever is necessary to make that transition. If there is a smooth and easy transition,* *repeat the process for anchors #2 and #3. Test by firing anchor #1. Be sure to release anchor #1 before the internal state you have anchored peaks.*

Step 9. *When B is satisfied the chain is complete, ask A to think of the limiting feeling. Just before the feeling peaks, fire anchor #1. The chain should follow automatically. Test by having A think of the limiting feeling again. This should take him through the chain.*

Step 10. *Future pace by having A identify a situation that has not happened, but might, that in the past would have produced the limiting feeling. Have him go through that experience in his imagination, noticing how it is different from what he would have predicted. The future pace will help to generalize the chain.*

Step 11. *Reverse roles and repeat steps 1 – 10.*

Sub-modalities were used here to diminish a feeling that limited or inhibited a person's behavior. That feeling, in its diminished state, was replaced by a feeling associated with a resource state. The feeling of the resource state was then intensified. In the future, as this person encounters situations that have produced the feeling that inhibited him, that feeling will set off the chain, the transition to the resource feeling being intensified. It is the movement towards possibility that allows a generalizing effect to take place so that the change is not confined to one event or to one context but spreads through a range of behaviors.

The SWISH PATTERN is a format that accomplishes the same thing as the chain, but with greater precision and economy. What follows is a demonstration by Richard of a standard swish pattern. This format will work in the majority of cases and is presented here as a model. You will notice that Richard sets up the pattern in such a way that three things change at the same time: size, brightness and going from associated to dissociated. It is the simultaneous change in those three parameters that builds a solid and stable configuration.

R.B. Think of something you would like to change. Something where you have a feeling, something you see or hear and you get a feeling that you have to behave in ways you don't like. You wouldn't act the way you did if you didn't have the feeling that you do. For example, if you show some people chocolate cake, they feel out of control. If they didn't feel out of control, they wouldn't eat more chocolate cake than they want to. It is not a question of whether they are good feelings or bad feelings; it is just that the person doesn't like having them. This is especially true when the feelings compel them to act in ways they do not like, in ways that do not fit with their consistent image of themselves as adult human beings. Now, do you have anything like that?

A. Yes.

R.B. Close your eyes and see what you would be seeing if you were actually there. Does it give you that feeling?

A. Yeah, it feels... ohhhh

R.B.   So it works. This is my way of knowing it is not an overwhelming phobia. You didn't scream and fall out of the chair. Now, make a big, bright, square image of what you would see if you were there. Put a border around it. Make it real bright and notice as you make it brighter if it becomes more intense.

A.   (nods)

R.B.   So she sits here feeling horrible. This is a demonstration that you can get people to do anything. Enough pain for one day. Come on back. That's right. Moving right along here. Now, what I want you to do is make an image in which you see yourself as if you had already made this change. As you see yourself having already made this change, how does that feel? Do you like that better?

A.   Yes.

R.B.   You do? You're sure?

A.   Positive.

R.B.   It doesn't have to be perfect. The question is, do you like it better? Go back and look at yourself that way again. Okay. Would you rather have that? Okay. Now, I want you to listen closely. Open your eyes. I'm going to give you instructions and I don't want you doing this while I am giving you instructions. In the first image, you saw what you saw at the time the event was occurring. In the second image, you saw yourself behaving in a way that was different, in a way that you liked. Let me repeat. In the first image, you are seeing it as if you are actually in the experience. The feelings you don't like are attached to that image. In the second image, you see yourself behaving the way you want to. The feelings you like are attached to that image. Shrink that picture down until it is just a little, tiny dark picture. Then take the first image, the one with the border around it, the one that makes you feel bad, and place that little, tiny dark picture, the one you like, down in the corner. Make the big one real bright and the little, tiny one in the corner dark. Then I want you to simply let the big one slowly begin to get darker as this little one down here gets bigger and brighter until it completely covers the other one. The first picture is so dark it disappears and all you see is the second picture. Then stop making pictures and open your eyes as a way to clear the screen. Start again at the beginning with the picture that had the bad feelings attached to it. That picture gets darker while the little one in the corner gets big and bright and completely covers the first image. I want you to do that five times... fast.

A.   I'm not sure...

R.B.   You see yourself in the little dark picture in the corner being the way you want and you see what you'd see in the big, bright one that makes you feel bad. Bright one gets darker. Little one gets bigger and brighter. Do that five times.

A.   Okay.

R.B.   One. There you go. Do it again, quick. Two. Once more. Three. And again. Five. Simple, right? Now, when you sat down here, you looked at an image—you saw something that made you feel bad. Look at it now. How does it make you feel?

A.   I'm not feeling much about it now.

R.B.   You're not feeling much. Well, look at it again.

A.   I'm not sure I can... I can't. It's just not there.

R.B.   Well, I believe you. You can think of another time when something happened where you had this feeling. You must have had it more than once if it bothered you.

A.   Yes.

R.B.   Look at it... and when you see that, how does it make you feel?

A.   Feel okay.

R.B.   This is something that is going to happen again in the real world. Close you eyes and see what you would see if it was going to happen again. Find out what happens. Whooosh.

A.   That's what happened. The picture I was looking at faded out and I saw myself behaving the way I like.

R.B.   The nice thing about this is that when you do encounter this in the real world, the external image doesn't go away, but what does happen is it makes you feel the way the second one does.

It is a mental strain to do the swish pattern, but once you have done it you have programmed your brain.

When you go back to the image that made you feel bad, there is a force that literally moves you in a different direction. That is why the speed at which you make the change is important. Once you begin the process, you do not allow the old configuration to stabilize but keep it in motion. The old feeling begins with the first image and simultaneously diminishes as the picture fades and the resource image and its associated feeling intensify and completely replace the first. It is the simultaneous utilization of the analog distinctions of size and brightness combined with the digital distinction of association/dissociation that result in a new, stable configuration. That is what we did in the last exercise with the anchor chain. The swish pattern is easier, quicker and much more explicit. Finally, it is the repetition that sets the pattern and makes it automatic. When an event stimulates the old feeling, the new pattern takes over and whooosh... the person feels differently and is capable of responding in a different way.

One of the essential ingredients in the swish pattern is that the person sees himself behaving the way he wants to behave in the context of a remembered event. Consider, for a moment, the different impact of a remembered event when you are associated and when you are dissociated. In this case, being associated in the remembered event is the image to which the bad, unwanted feelings are attached. The swish pattern diminishes those feelings by dimming the first image. If the person were to associate in the second image, he would re-access the unwanted feelings. By holding the second image dissociated, he is able to go through the event accessing only the feelings of the resource state.

Being dissociated from the way you want to be also puts you in a meta position relative to change. Not only does seeing yourself having made the change feel good, but you can feel good about feeling good. It is this meta position that makes the image of how you want to behave an impelling one and sets the direction for a whole new set of behaviors that will move you toward its fulfillment.

A critical element in using the swish pattern effectively is the structure of the transition to the feelings of the resource state. In the standard model Richard demonstrated, brightness is used to diminish unwanted feelings and to simultaneously intensify wanted feelings. At the same time the associated image is being dimmed (diminishing feelings) the dissociated image is being brightened (intensifying feelings). The transitional structure has to work that way.

One woman, who had an unpleasant experience in a dark alley, intensified the feelings of the resource states as she brightened the dissociated image. However, the bad feelings were intensified when she darkened the associated image; the alley got darker and more frightening. In this instance, brightness will not affect the desired transition. Distance did provide a mechanism to simultaneously diminish the unwanted feeling while intensifying the wanted feelings. The first, associated image moved off into the distance (diminishing the feelings) and the second image moved closer (intensifying the feelings) at the same time. The first image disappeared in the distance while the second image got closer and bigger until it filled her frame.

Since this next exercise is one in which you will utilize the swish pattern, check to be sure that the analog sub-modalities work the same on both sides of the equation. In other words, as you increase the brightness, the feelings of both the associated and dissociated images are intensified.

EXERCISE: THE SWISH PATTERN

In threes. Person C acts as a resource for A and B.

Step 1. *Person A identifies something he would like to change. When some particular event takes place, he gets a feeling that causes him to behave in ways he does not like.*

Step 2. *A closes his eyes and sees what he would be seeing if he were there in the event. Notice whether this produces the feeling. If not, pick something else. If it does produce the feeling, interrupt the pattern to enable A to clear his screen.*

Step 3. *B instructs A to make a big, bright, square picture of what he would see if he were there. Be sure A has a border around the picture. B then instructs A to make the picture brighter and notices, as he brightens the image, if his feelings become more intense. If not, check with A and explore alternative sub-modalities to find a suitable mechanism. If they do intensify, interrupt the pattern to get rid of those unpleasant feelings.*

Step 4. *B instructs A to make a picture in which he sees himself as if he had already made the change. Question A as to whether or not he likes the feelings generated by that image. B and C calibrate to A's response.*

Step 5. *A, with his eyes open, is instructed by B in the manner in which the transition is to be made.*

"In the first image, you saw what you saw at the time the event was occurring. In the second image, you saw yourself behaving in a way that was different, in a way that you liked. Shrink the picture in which you see yourself behaving the way you like until it is a little dark picture. Then take the first image, the one with the border around it, and put the little one in the corner. The big picture is bright and the little one is dark. Then let the big picture slowly begin to get dark while the little one gets big and bright, bigger and brighter until it completely covers the other image. First picture is so dark it disappears and all you see is the second one. Then stop making pictures and open your eyes as a way to clear your screen. Do that one time."

Step 6. *Check to be sure A understood the instructions and was able to carry them out.*

Step 7. *B and C watch closely as A repeats the swish fives times fast, taking no longer that it takes to say 'whooossssh' to make the transition. B and C are watching, calibrating to A's responses to see if he achieves the intensity of the resource state he reached in Step 4.*

Step 8. *Pattern interrupt. Then test by having A look at the image that produced the feelings he had when he first identified the change he wanted to make.*

Step 9. *Future pace by asking A to close his eyes and see what he would see if this were going to happen again.*

Step 10. *Change roles and repeat so that each of you has an opportunity to function in each role.*

Sub-modalities have been used here to change behavior by changing the feelings associated with memories. They can also be used to change your present experience. There are lots of times when we are having fun, sort of, but life would be more of a party if we were able to pump up that feeling of fun, making it stronger. You did something similar to this in Chapter 1 in an exercise called, "Making Things Better Than They Should Have Been." That was an instance in which you simply substituted one set of sub-modalities for another. This exercise utilizes a mechanism similar to the swish pattern. It also functions like stacking anchors, so that each repetition is more intense.

*EXERCISE: USING SUB-MODALITIES TO
          CHANGE THE PRESENT STATE*

Individually.

Step 1. *Close your eyes and see on the inside what you saw when they were open. This creates a memory for where you are now. You may have to repeat the process several times, opening and closing your eyes, until you have an image of the present situation.*

Step 2. *Put a very small picture in the center of that image. A small picture in which you see yourself right where you are sitting, having exquisitely more fun.*

Step 3. *Then, whooossh, open that little picture up from the middle. This is like some of the TV* *special effects where a new picture opens up from the center and completely replaces the first.*

Step 4. *Step inside the picture so that you are seeing what you would see if you were actually there.*

Step 5. *As soon as you step inside the picture, another little picture opens up from the middle in which you see yourself sitting there having even more fun. Repeat ten times, fast, real fast.*

It's not so hard to have fun. You can use the same process to intensify any resource state. Just think; you never have to be bored again: just start pumping up curiosity. You might even become curious about what would be different if there was a change in the angle of view with each of the pictures that opens up from the middle. Does a change in the point of view intensify the resource state more or less than using the same point of view?

Up to this point, we have been dealing with specific events, memories of experiences we have had and the feelings associated with those memories. However, much of our behavior stems from our beliefs about ourselves and about the world we live in. We don't think much about them or question them as a rule, but they operate as guiding principles. It is what we believe that gives our lives a stability and a sense of continuity. Beliefs are so important to us as human beings that we are willing to go to war to uphold them. In fact, much of our behavior is devoted to maintaining or reinforcing our beliefs.

No matter how important they are, we have all held beliefs that we no longer believe. People convert to another religion, change political affiliation, get married and divorced all because of changing beliefs. The issue is not to devalue beliefs, but simply to view them less rigidly. Beliefs not only can and do change, but there is a structure to what we believe, a structure in the way in which we believe what we do.

Take a few minutes now to identify a belief you have about yourself that imposes some limitation on your behavior, that inhibits you from trying new things that you think would be fun, exciting, or challenging. You can think of it as a belief that keeps life from being more of a party. There are a lot of beliefs that are worth having, so choose carefully what you want to change about what you believe about yourself.

Identifying a belief about yourself that you want to change will make the following transcript of Richard working with beliefs more meaningful.

R.B.   Do you have a belief about yourself that fits that category?

E.   A limiting belief?

R.B.   I mean you have a belief and if it weren't true, there is something you would rather believe than that but you don't. You got one of those? Okay. How do you know you're having it? I mean, you have more than one belief, so you have got to be able to tell them apart.

E.   Constrict...

R.B.   But how do you know which belief?

E.   I see a picture of, uummmm...

R.B.   Don't be telling us what's in it. We don't want to be knowing about your content here. Start telling people about content and they get lost. Now, I want you to stop and think of something that could be one way or the other. For instance, you might have dinner at home tonight or you might go to a restaurant—doesn't matter. Could be one way or the other. Got anything like that? Okay. How are the two beliefs different? Is, for example, one located in a different place than the other?

E.   Yeah. The belief I don't want is over to the left and the other is straight ahead and higher.

R.B.   Does one perhaps have sound?

E.   Yeah, the belief has sound.

R.B.   Alright. Is there any other differences between them? You remember sub-modalities? Do they both have movement? Is one bigger than the other? Are they both in color? Are they both the same distance away?

E.   The belief is smaller than the wishy-washy one. It's farther away. There is no movement in the belief and they're both in color.

R.B.   Okay. Now I tell you what I want you to do. I want you to take all the content from the strong belief, I want you to push it off in the distance and I want you to snap it back so that it has all the characteristics of the wishy-washy one. Location. But before you do that... old pattern interruption here. There must be a belief you'd rather have in its place.

E.   Yes.

R.B.   Generally, the one people want is the opposite of what they don't want. Be sure you think of this in positive terms and that it be a process and not a goal. For instance, if you were just learning to ski and started to believe you were an advanced skier, that's a good way to get killed. But it is useful for you to believe that you have an aptitude for skiing and that you can learn to ski quickly, easily, and well, and that you can enjoy the learning. Can you think about that new belief in those terms?

E.   Yes. Putting it in those terms makes it much more real already.

R.B.   Rushing ahead again. One more thing first. It is called an ecology check. If you were to believe this about yourself, how would it affect your life? If you were to believe this about yourself, how would it affect those close to you, your work, your family? Is there any need to modify the belief so it is more appropriate? Would having this belief conflict with your values?

E.   No. No, it's okay.

R.B.   Okay. Now, put that new belief where the wishy-washy one is.

E.   The belief that I want?

R.B.   Yeah. So that when you (snaps fingers) move the belief that is strong now, you can snap back the other way and put something in its place. Concept is to create a void and fill it. The reason you move it to wishy-washy first is so that you have something. Right now, that new belief is something you don't have, but wishy-washy at least makes it a possibility.

E. Wow. I can...

R.B. Alright. Now, take the old belief and move it off in the distance (snaps fingers) and (snaps fingers) bring it back so it's wishy-washy. Then (snaps fingers) put the new one in its place, wherever the strong belief was. You want the new belief to be a strong one. Complete with sound. *All* the characteristics. There you go. Whhooosh. Just helping. Alright. You remember the belief you used to have that was strong? How do you feel about it now?

E. Neehhh.

R.B. Neehhh. Okay. What about the one you like? Is that a strong belief?

E. Yeah.

R.B. Make it bigger and brighter.

E. Feels good. I can't believe it was that easy.

Most beliefs about self are a function of generalization: specific events are generalized to the category of self. Having failed to do something after half a dozen tries, a person then begins to believe he is incapable of doing it. If a child is told repeatedly that he is stupid or clumsy, he begins to believe he is stupid or clumsy. The belief becomes part of a self-concept. The ugly duckling story would be more accurate if the ugly duckling became a beautiful swan but continued to think of himself as ugly.

Robert Dilts tells the story of a man who believed he was a corpse. His psychiatrist, in an effort to prove the belief wrong, asked if corpses bleed. The man said, "No, they do not." The man then agreed to an experiment, and the good doctor pricked his finger with a needle. The man looked at his bleeding finger and said, "I was wrong, corpses do bleed." However fixed the belief may be, there is still a conceptual configuration that maintains it, and it is that configuration that is subject to change. The structure of the change is similar to the swish pattern: the present state is diminished and the desired state is intensified. The mechanism, apart from the use of sub-modalities, is to create possibilities in both directions through the use of the wishy-washy belief. This is not a weak belief, but something that you do not care about one way or the other. It could be this or that and either way it does not matter.

The rigidity of the strong belief the person has and does not want is loosened, is made into a possibility by changing its sub-modalities to those of wishy-washy. Once that change is made, the possibility that "it doesn't matter" begins to formulate. The belief the person wants and does not have is also made into a possibility through the sub-modality changes to that of wishy-washy. In the demonstration transcript, when E. made that change, she exclaimed, "Wow, I can..." The feeling of the desired state had already begun to express itself.

In the belief change, the pattern is a sequenced rather than a simultaneous change as it is in the swish pattern, but the speed with which the change is made remains critical. Richard snapped his fingers and added the "whooosh" to direct the speed of the changes. The old configuration is kept in movement until a new configuration has stabilized. The spatial location of images and sounds is so impactful in the belief change that once the spatial shift has been made, with the other sub-modality changes accompanying the spatial shift, it is virtually impossible to put those images and sounds into their old configuration. It is the stabilizing influence of location plus the fact that both the old, strong belief and the new, wanted belief are included in the configuration that allows the belief change to take place with one run.

EXERCISE: CHANGING A BELIEF

In threes. Person C, in the meta position, takes notes and provides a resource to Person B.

Step 1. *Person A identifies some belief about himself he does not like, some belief that if he did not have it, he would have more behavioral flexibility—more choices. He does not share the content of the belief with B and C.*

Step 2. *Person B elicits the sub-modalities of the strong, unwanted belief.*

Step 3. *A then identifies some choice in which either alternative is acceptable, such as, "I might have fish and chips for lunch or I might find something else on the menu that would be more appealing. It doesn't matter which I choose." This is the belief called wishy-washy.*

Step 4. *B elicits the sub-modalities of wishy-washy.*

Step 5. *B then takes A through the sub-modalities of the unwanted belief, changing them one at a time into the sub-modalities of wishy-washy. Determine which change makes the biggest difference. Be sure to return the sub-modalities back to their original form before going on to make the next change.*

Step 6. *A then identifies a belief he would like to have that would be more useful than the old belief. This new belief is set in positive terms, is considered as a process and not as a goal. Include an ecology check: how would his having this belief affect others, his work? Is this belief consistent with his values and the values of those who are close to him? If necessary, modify the new belief to meet these conditions.*

Step 7. *Shift the new belief to the sub-modalities of wishy-washy.*

Step 8. *Then (using the notes from Step 5) B instructs A in how to diminish the old, strong belief and then to bring it back as wishy-washy. For instance, if the sub-modality that made the greatest change in Step 5 was distance, B would instruct A to move the old belief off in the distance and then to bring it back to the same distance as wishy-washy.*

Step 9. *Then snap the new belief (pictures and sounds) into the configuration of the old belief.*

Step 10. *Test and future pace. B asks A what he believes about himself now. If A has this new belief, what will he be doing that he could not do before? A runs a sequence of the new behavior.*

Note: *Use pattern interruptions between each of the steps in the exercise to ensure that each step in the process is clean. Also, keep in mind that the speed with which the person makes the changes is critical in effecting the belief change.*

Structuring the new belief in positive terms and as a process serves much the same function as being dissociated from where you want to be in the swish pattern. The new belief becomes impelling and draws the person toward the behavior that is consistent with the belief. The belief change, then, like the swish pattern, results in generative change. Although the change is made with a specific belief, the new pattern generalizes cross-contextually to promote new behaviors that direct the person toward the realization of his potential. The belief change has set a direction for his behavior that is expanding rather than limiting.

However impelling the new behavior may be, people sometimes need further assistance in making the transition from their old behavioral patterns to the new. It is something they cannot do in one step and need a structured transition from one to the other. In one workshop a person said, "I really want to engage in the new behavior but I think perhaps I don't know enough so I hold back instead of going for it." The feeling he has is termed 'hesitation.'

He has a feeling, 'hesitation,' which is connected to a justification. Justifications are both valid and invalid. The justification here is, "I don't know enough." That is an interesting statement. What does "I don't know enough" mean? Is it the opposite of "I do know enough?"

"Don't" is *doing not: do* plus the conjunction *not*. There-fore, I do, that is, I engage in the activity of not... In this case, the person is engaged in the activity of not knowing enough. The functional part of this is how he does "not know enough." Not knowing enough here is an active process. What he said was that he holds back, he hesi-tates. In order to manufacture the feeling of *hesitation*, he has to engage in the activity of not knowing enough. One way to deal with that would be to explore the structure of hesitation. Another possibility is to use *hesitation* as the first link in a chain.

A chain is a sequence of transitional steps that are easy and natural that will move a person from one internal state to another. In this case, we have to estab-lish a series of transitional steps that will lead him from *hesitation* to *going for it*. The chain we will use here is as follows:

hesitation
frustration
impatience
wanton desire
going for it

You established a chain with kinesthetic anchors, enhanced by sub-modalities, in the first exercise in this chapter. In this next exercise, you will set the chain using sub-modalities only.

EXERCISE: CHAINING DIRECTLY WITH SUB-MODALITIES

In threes. Person C takes careful notes of the sub-modalities elicited.

Step 1. Person A identifies some experience he had in which he hesitated seeing what he saw and hearing what he heard at the time.

Step 2. Person B elicits the sub-modalities of A's experience of hesitation.

Step 3. A then finds an example of frustration, some experience in which he was frustrated, again seeing what he saw and hearing what he heard.

Step 4. B elicits the sub-modalities of frustration. C notes only those that are different from hesitation. What you are looking for is how the sub-modalities change between states.

Step 5. Next, find an example of impatience and compare the sub-modalities of impatience with frustration. C notes the differences between the two.

Step 6. Then find the differences between impatience and wanton desire.

Step 7. Then find the differences between wanton desire and going for it.

Step 8. B then instructs A in using the structure of the swish pattern to create the chain. You will have four sets of sub-modality changes that will move the feelings of the experience of hesitation through the sequence: hesitation, frustration, impatience, wanton desire, going for it.

The content of the experience of hesitation is held constant throughout the sequence being swished. The person is associated in the image being swished from and dissociated in the image being swished to. For instance, A sees what he saw at the time when he hesitated. That is a big square *picture with a border around it. The little picture in the corner, which gets bigger and brighter as the first image fades out, is a picture in which he sees himself in the same experience but with the sub-modality distinctions of frustration. A then steps into that image, seeing the event as if it were happening with the sub-modalities of frustration, and another image gets big and bright in which he sees himself in the same scene but with the sub-modalities of impatience. The same process is continued through wanton desire and going for it.*

Step 9. *Test and future pace.*

Step 10. *Change roles.*

This puts the pieces together, utilizing the differences in the sub-modalities of each state. The chain also sets a direction, and what you end up with is something that is long-lasting and will generalize to other areas of life. Since we are in the playground of NLP, let's explore another way to accomplish the sub-modality changes necessary to establish a chain. In the last exercise, you utilized the structure of the swish pattern. Here you are going to accomplish the same sub-modality shifts by utilizing an analog distinction.

The structure of the swish pattern and the other sub-modality interventions thus far has been to diminish the unwanted feeling while the wanted feeling is intensified. The unwanted feeling is not changed, it is simply diminished. In the threshold pattern, the unwanted feeling is changed. An analog distinction, which will intensify the unwanted feeling, is increased very quickly. In doing this the unwanted feeling becomes stronger and stronger and suddenly changes. Because the feeling the person does · not like is intensified, it is necessary to do this very quickly, otherwise he will tend to stop and remain stuck in the bad feeling. As an example of this, if brightness intensifies the unwanted feeling, very quickly brighten the image, making it brighter and brighter until the feeling changes. The pattern of image/feeling seems to simply disappear.

If you use the threshold structure by itself, it is useful to have people then shift the analog back with an image in which they see themselves as they would like to be in that experience. The little boy with the snake phobia had a recurrence of troublesome snake images. He had been watching a TV horror movie and was scared by it. Not wanting to continue watching, he switched channels to a program in which someone was being attacked by a snake. The interesting thing here is that the images that later frightened him were constructions and not memories. I had him take one of those images and begin to brighten it slowly. That intensified the feelings. Then he dimmed the image and quickly brightened it so bright he could no longer see it. The feeling disappeared. Then he dimmed the screen and saw an image of himself with all of the sub-modality characteristics of a time when he felt comfortable, safe and secure. Not only did that eliminate the snake fantasies at bedtime, but he was reassured to know he had a technique he could apply if they should recur at some later time.

EXERCISE: CHAINING DIRECTLY WITH SUB-MODALITIES (A VARIATION)

In threes. The same group as in the last exercise.

Step 1. *Go through the notes from the last exercise and find an analog distinction that varies between the different states. You may end with one analog distinction that varies throughout the sequence, or you may have a different analog variable with each pair.*

Step 2. *B will take A through the sequence, utilizing the analog variables. For instance, if brightness is an analog distinction between hesitation and frustration, A will see what he saw/hear what he heard in the experience of hesitation, then begin to turn up the brightness until the image whites out, then dim the brightness to the same level as frustration in which he will see himself in the same experience with all of the sub-modality characteristics of frustration... both analog and digital distinctions.*

Use the analog to push the experience to threshold so that you can move to the next step gracefully. B will take A through the sequence slowly the first time so that A learns how to do it.

Step 3. *B will now take A through the sequence again, fast. Push him a little faster than is comfortable.*

We have used the chain here to take a person from a state of immobility to a state where he is ready to take appropriate action. In this exercise it was called 'hesitation' to 'going for it,' but there are many states of immobility that people experience. Phrases like writer's block or creative block come to mind. You may want to experiment some with the different steps in the chain, given a particular present state and desired state. States of consciousness such as boredom, curiosity, anticipation, excitement, humor, confusion (mild) and creative are all useful. What makes the chain as effective a mechanism as it is is the utilization of the spontaneous changes in sub-modalities people make as they shift from state to state. In the exercises you have just explored, you were utilizing those spontaneous changes deliberately to effect a behavioral change.

The swish pattern you have used is a general model, but that model can be tailored to duplicate what a person does spontaneously to achieve some particular limitation. When the mechanism of the limiting pattern is utilized to make the change, the effect will be even more powerful than the standard swish. This next exercise provides a structure for the development of a swish pattern designed for the particular mechanism of the person you are working with.

EXERCISE: TAILORING THE SWISH PATTERN TO THE INDIVIDUAL

In pairs.

Step 1. *Person A identifies a limitation, something she considers a problem that she wants to change.*

Step 2. *Person B gets A to teach him how to have her problem. Be specific about how you would know when to have the problem and how you would generate the problem/feeling state.*

One of the most effective ways to accomplish this is to ask, "Suppose you wanted to take a vacation from being you and I was going to fill in for you for the day, I would have to have your limitation. How would I know when to have it? What would I have to do inside my head in order to have this problem?" This presupposes the limitation is an achievement and can be taught to someone else. *(See "Anticipatory Loss" in* MAGIC IN ACTION, *Richard Bandler, META Publications.)*

Step 3. *As B elicits the strategy by which A generates the problem state, he identifies at least two visual sub-modalities that change the intensity and quality of her feelings. Things like size and distance, brightness and clarity, shape and location, direction and speed of movement are examples. Test your conclusions by having her make the same sub-modality changes with another image and notice how her feelings change in relation to the sub-modality changes with the new image content.*

Step 4. *Once B has two analog distinctions that are most important in creating the problem state, he instructs A to see herself as if she had already made the change she wants. She must see herself in this picture. Go for behavioral changes that are really impelling. This should be an image that she looks at and says, "Oh God, if I could only be like that." The stronger the feelings generated by that second image, the more effective the change will be.*

Step 5. *Design a swish using the analog distinctions B identified as being most important in creating the problem state. As an example, if the critical sub-modalities are size and distance, the* *first image is a large, close picture in which she sees what she saw at the time. The second image, in which she sees herself as if she had made the change, is small and far away. Large, close image moves off into the distance getting smaller and smaller while the small image of the desired state moves closer and gets bigger and bigger. B instructs A in the swish and establishes that she is able to accomplish the sub-modality changes.*

Step 6. *A then repeats the swish five times fast. Each time she completes a step, she stops making pictures and clears her screen to begin again with the problem state image.*

Step 7. *Test and future pace.*

Step 8. *Change roles.*

What makes this tailored swish so powerful is that you are utilizing the sub-modality patterns the person has already learned. In the past, these are the patterns that produced the unwanted state. As you have heard so often, "People are not broken; the structure of what they do works perfectly." Here you were using that perfected structure to generate a more useful response. The swish creates a direction, a movement toward an impelling image so that the person continues to strive to become what he wants.

The exercises presented here are merely examples of what is possible. You do not have only one limitation you want to change. The swish pattern provides a way for you to change as many of them as you want. The more you use it, the more skill and flexibility you will develop. The exercise required you to work with the visual sub-modalities because the visual system enables you to vary two images simultaneously. It is much more difficult to hear more than one sound at a time. However, as you develop your skill and flexibility with the visual, you will be able to adapt the patterns to other systems.

In the same way that you can use the swish pattern to eliminate limitations, the belief change can be used to change those beliefs that, if you did not believe them but the opposite, life would be more pleasurable and more productive. Start making a list of the things you want to change, adding to it any limitations or beliefs that get in your way. A lot of people think they are going to fail and so they don't try. If something cannot be done, you don't need to worry about it because you just won't be able to do it. This knowledge takes the worry out of everything. So, if you make yourself believe something that is not true, that you can do anything, then you will find out what you can do. You will get a lot more done than most people. When you create a belief that you can do things and that the process is going to be fun, when you connect learning with fun, you will do a lot more of it.

In certain situations a lot of people experience what they describe as reticence. Reticence is similar to hesitation but more closely related to the way a person thinks about himself. Hesitation is justified by things like, "I just don't know enough." Reticence, on the other hand, is accompanied by statements like, "It would be fun to do that, but that's just not the kind of person I am." One thing that is sure about reticence is that it eats up time. Perhaps you would like to have more intimacy in your relationships, or to be more relaxed and spontaneous in public, or you would like to try something you have never done before. Each time you think about one of those things, you say to yourself, "I could never do that." Well, this next exercise will give you a choice about being the kind of person you want to be.

EXERCISE: ELIMINATING RETICENCE, OR NOT

In pairs.

Step 1. *Person A identifies some behavior that she would like to engage in, but as she thinks about doing it she feels reticent.*

Step 2. *Person B asks her, "Where do you want to be?" B uses his information-gathering skills to assist A in developing a well-formed outcome.*

Step 3. *B instructs A to make a clear image of the new behavior in which she sees herself doing what she would like to do. Actually this is a sequence of behaviors, a little movie in which A sees herself engaged in an activity that is something she wants. Be sure that A is able to see the whole sequence.*

Step 4. *Then A sees what she currently does in the same or similar circumstances. This is an associated image and is complete with the internal dialogue and the tonality that accompanies it. It is as if she were actually doing the behavior.*

Step 5. *B elicits a sub-modality comparison. What is the difference between the two sets of images. Look for differences in size, brightness, location, distance, clarity... things like that.*

Step 6. *A then identifies another experience in the same or similar circumstance that is the closest example she can find to a time when she was* *playing. B elicits the sub-modalities of that experience, again looking for differences between the sub-modalities of the play experience and the other two.*

Step 7. *A then looks at the desired state image, seeing the parts she wants, then she steps inside the picture, becoming associated. Does she like the way that feels? B asks her to compare that with what she is doing now in those circumstances and to pick the one she wants. If A wants what she already has, fine. If she wants what she has created, the process is a simple one.*

Step 8. *Using A's belief strategy, B assists her to make a belief change. A has created something she wants and has compared that with something she believes; "that's the way it is." All that she has to do is to switch them so that she believes what she has created. In this case, to vary the process and make it more interesting, use the sub-modalities elicited in the play experience in place of wishy-washy as a way of creating possibilities.*

It will be interesting to find out what happens. You may surprise and delight yourselves with new behaviors you never thought possible. After all, that is what a new behavior generator is for. Having a range of behaviors that you like, whether they are new or old, is fine, but there is a quality that we can add to our experiences that transforms them from wonderful to ecstatic. We can call that quality 'sizzle.' Jazz musicians refer to that same quality as being "in the groove."

EXERCISE: ADDING SIZZLE TO YOUR RESPONSES

In threes.

Step 1. *Person A identifies those moments in his life when things were going so perfectly that he felt if he put his finger in the air sparks would jump because there was so much static electricity in the moment. Think of the magic moments when everything was clicking perfectly. It can be anything: for those of you who have children, perhaps it was that first time you saw your new-born child; maybe it was a time when you were in love; it could have been an athletic event where your responses were honed by months of practice; or a dance where the dancer was danced. It can be anything where the experience was so magical that the air around you crackled with the energy you generated.*

Step 2. *Person B is going to be anchoring A's responses. When you are eliciting A's responses, be sure that they are intense responses. The intensity of his response is going to be directly related to the congruity you demonstrate: voice tone, facial expressions, posture, gestures. Pace your partner and lead him to an even more intense response. This makes it easier to anchor and much more useful.*

B instructs A to see what he saw and hear what he heard at the time he was in one of those magical moments. Then, using sub-modalities, instruct him to make it bigger, brighter, closer—whatever can be utilized here to intensify the experience. Anchor it.

This submodality list will vary slightly with each person. To begin with, elicit the sub-modalities of the sizzle experience and find out which sub-modality changes will amplify the experience the most.

Step 3. *Each time B is able to elicit more of a sizzle response, anchor it in the same place, stacking the anchors for sizzle.*

Step 4. *A then picks out three things he wants to be able to do. Then B will instruct A in the following steps for each of those activities.*

    a. Person A sees himself doing the activity. B fires the sizzle anchor and holds it throughout the sequence.

    b. Person A then associates in the experience, seeing and hearing what he would be seeing and hearing if he was actually doing it. B fires the sizzle anchor and holds it throughout this sequence.

    c. Person A then gets up and engages in the activity in a role play with Person C. B fires the sizzle anchor and holds it through this future pace.

Step 5. *Person A makes his own sizzle anchor so that when he sees somebody doing something that looks like fun, something he would like to do himself, he can incorporate the behavior and sizzle it up into another of those magic times.*

3 Scratching the Surface

Perhaps the most elusive of the sub-modality systems is the kinesthetic because it is the one system of which we are most aware. However, that awareness tends to be non-specific. Our attention is directed toward the culmination of a sequence of body sensations rather than the sequence itself: we are aware of the end product but not of the process that produced it.

By now you are familiar with sounds that get louder or higher in pitch, with images that get bigger and brighter, and with the impact of these sub-modality shifts on the intensity and quality of experience. What you are about to explore in this chapter is the impact of body sensation itself on the intensity and quality of experience.

EXERCISE: EXPLORING KINESTHETIC SUB-MODALITIES

In pairs.

Step 1. *Person A identifies a pleasant experience.*

Step 2. *Person B, using the sub-modality list from Table 2, instructs A in changing the kinesthetic sub-modalities of the experience. Be sure to have A return the sub-modality he has changed back into its original form before going on to the next.*

Step 3. *Identify the critical kinesthetic sub-modalities. Also notice which kinesthetic changes effect the visual and auditory systems the most. Pay particular attention to those visual and auditory changes that are most difficult to change.*

Step 4. *Change roles.*

Step 5. *Repeat Step 1 – 3 with an unpleasant experience and note the difference, if any.*

Let's go back to beginnings and to the language patterns that carry the implicit descriptions of our experience. We are all familiar with expressions like, "I'm feeling out of balance"; "I need to get centered"; "walking tall"; "the responsibility weighs heavily"; "he's just spinning his wheels"; "the effect is dizzying." It is a long list of kinesthetic references and you can begin now to pay attention to predicate phrases that define some aspect of body sensation.

There are two exercises that are particularly useful in developing a greater kinesthetic awareness. The first is a gestalt exercise in sensory awareness; the second is the NLP exercise in requisite variety. They are both capable of producing a trance state and you may find it useful to set a strong here-and-now anchor to enable you to return to a present, waking reality quickly and easily.

EXERCISE: GESTALT BODY AWARENESS

Singly.

Step 1. *Set a here-and-now anchor.*

Step 2. *Sit or lie down comfortably. As you become aware of body sensations, say to yourself, "Now I am aware of...", and with the next sensation, "Now I am aware of..." At the beginning, concentrate only on those sensations on the outside of your body: the weight of your body lying on the bed, the feeling of your clothing, the feeling of your breath on your lips as you exhale, the pressure of your heels, the temperature of your body or body parts.*

Step 3. *Continue step 1, but add whatever you are aware of internally: a tension in your abdomen, an itch on your right cheek, a tingling in your left leg. Notice whether you are equally aware of all parts of your body or whether there are some areas in which there is little or no sensation. With each new awareness, repeat, "Now I am aware of..." Keep the process going for 10 – 15 minutes. If you find yourself drifting off and thinking about other things, simply remind yourself of the task and again begin to be aware of body sensation.*

EXERCISE: REQUISITE VARIETY

Singly.

Step 1. *Set a here-and-now anchor.*

Step 2. *Select a color. Then visualize a content-free field of that color. As if, for example, you were totally immersed in the color blue.*

Step 3. *Begin to notice what sound (again, content-free) accompanies that color. Hear the sound, allowing it to become appropriately loud and clear.*

Step 4. *Begin to notice the body sensation(s) that accompany the color and the sound. Notice if there is movement to the sensation and where in your body you are most aware of the sensation.*

Step 5. *Repeat, selecting a different color or hue. Continue until you have explored the variation with six colors.*

The more you practice these exercises, the finer the distinctions you can make. Some of you may have begun to experiment with variations in the intensity of the sensations and noticing how that affects your experience. You may be more aware now of the beginning of the sensation and its movement to the place where you are most aware. In Aikido, which in the opinion of some is the most elegant of the Japanese martial arts, the life force, or Ki, originates at a point roughly four inches below the navel. The Ki can not only be experienced as a body sensation, but can be intensified or diminished and directed throughout the body. Much of the art is directed toward the development of Ki and the practitioner's ability to control its flow and direction. In the same way that each experience has an accompanying breathing pattern, so does each experience have an accompanying body sensation. The flow and direction of that sensation can have a profound effect on the intensity and quality of the experience.

I have had clients who, while describing their present state, would accompany the description with a minute head rotation—generally clockwise. As they began to explore their desired states, I would ask them to reverse the movement of their heads. As soon as they began to rotate their heads in the other direction, their confusion began to clear up and they were able to see possibilities that were unavailable prior to the conscious head movement.

I worked with one man recently who complained of being nervous in crowds to the point of nausea. The nausea was so severe that he frequently had to vomit and found it almost impossible to be with friends in a restaurant or bar where he felt crowded. He had no awareness of visual or auditory sub-modalities and any memory of being in a crowd immediately produced the nausea. Since I had to work with what he was aware of, I started asking questions about what he was aware of just prior to the feeling of nausea. The nausea was preceded by a feeling of dizziness. The following transcript illustrates the kinesthetic intervention.

Will: What happens when you feel dizzy? What does it feel like?

Man: It's like the room starts to spin.

Will: Do it now and notice what happens.

Man: I don't like that.

Will: What happened?

Man: I started to get nauseous.

Will: Yes, but you stopped yourself. How did you do that?

Man: I stopped the room from spinning.

Will: So you've got control. That's good. Two's company and three's a crowd, but there's only two of us here, and you were still able to make yourself feel nauseous. Now, when you started the room spinning, did you feel nauseous right away or did you have to get it up to speed before the feeling of nausea began?

Man: It was right away, I think.

Will: Do it again and find out. This time start real slow and then begin to speed it up slowly until you begin to feel nauseous. Find out if the speed of the spinning makes a difference. Let me know when the nauseous feeling starts.

Man: I feel it now.

Will: It took a while before the feeling began. Do it again and this time speed it up even more. Make the room spin faster. And what happens?

Man: I feel like I'm going to puke.

Will: Stop it. What happens now?

Man: I still feel like puking.

Will: That's okay. It's a little like being seasick, only here the feeling of nausea is related to how fast the room is spinning. If you get it going fast enough, then the nausea takes over, and even if you stop the spinning, you still want to puke. One more time. By the way, before you start, which way does the room spin?

Man: To the right.

Will: Okay. Room spinning to the right, speed it up until you feel nauseous.

Man: (nods)

Will: Stop the spinning and begin to spin it the other way, to the left. And what happens?

Man: It went away.

Will: What went away?

Man: The feeling of wanting to puke.

Will: What about dizzy?

Man: That went away, too.

Will: You remember when you were a little kid and you would spin around until you got so dizzy you'd fall down? We all did that when we were kids. The first experimentation in mind-altering. Later you discovered that if you went to the right and then stopped just before you fell down and started to spin the other way, your sense of balance returned quickly and the feeling of dizziness was gone. Same thing here only you are doing it all on the inside. So, do it again. Find out that you really do have control over the process. Spin to the right, feel nauseous, stop, and spin to the left, feeling of

dizziness and nausea disappear, stop the spinning. See, whatever it is that happens, you've
learned to do one thing really well. This is an
opportunity to learn to do something else
equally well that is more useful.

Man: Is that something I have to practice?

Will: Sure, but with practice comes control, and
with control comes choice. You can make
yourself sick any time you want. If that serves
some useful purpose, go ahead and be sick.
The important thing is not whether you are
sick or not, the important thing is that you are
in control. So practice a couple of times now,
and then we get to go across the street and
have lunch in the deli.

He did fine in the deli and was able to enjoy his lunch
despite the fact that the place was noisy and crowded.
Whenever he found himself starting to spin, he would
simply move it in the other direction and eliminate the
feeling of dizziness. It has been my experience that a
person will choose the most useful behavior once he
discovers he really has a choice. In this case, the
unwanted behavior stopped after a couple of weeks. As
he said, "I don't have to do that any more."

The question is, what was spinning? His accessing
cues would indicate that the dizziness resulted from the
movement of internal images, but they remained out of
consciousness. The most interesting aspect is that he
was able to effect change without conscious awareness
of the content by changing the one thing of which he was

aware. Meet the client in the client's model of the world. Whatever that model may be, there are elements of it that can be utilized.

This next exercise comes from the theater and the work of Stanislavsky, but it is useful in establishing idiosyncratic anchors for ourselves. In the development of 'method acting,' Stanislavsky used the process to help the actor develop a complete and naturalistic character for the stage. What is important within the present context is that it relies on your own unique and special model of the world.

EXERCISE: DEVELOPING IDIOSYNCRATIC ANCHORS

In pairs.

Step 1. *Person A identifies an experience in which she was extremely competent. Since you have already done the 'sizzle' exercise, you should have access to a number of those magic times when everything you did was just right.*

Step 2. *Person B assists A in re-establishing the kinesthetic connection to that experience. What is the body sensation that accompanies that experience? Visual and auditory sub-modalities can be used to assist A in getting in touch with the feeling of the moment.*

Step 3. *A then identifies some kinesthetic element (posture, gesture, facial expression, pelvic angle) that is unique to the moment and one that she can duplicate. It may be useful here to have A demonstrate the kinesthetic component.*

Step 4. *When B is sure the kinesthetic component has been linked to the experience, he anchors it.*

Step 5. *Pattern interrupt and then fire the anchor and notice whether you get a corresponding physical shift in A. If not, reset the anchor.*

Step 6. *Future pace and fire the anchor. Future pace a second time without firing the anchor and notice if the physical shift occurs in the future experience.*

An example of the physical shift that can accompany this state is a client who was a bicycle racer. When he would begin a sprint, there was a slight forward hunch to his shoulders and a rounding of his back. When he repeated the movement, he experienced a surge of power throughout his body and a sense of exhilaration and well-being. His body had been conditioned to the sequence: shoulders forward and back rounded—pour it on! Anchoring and future pacing the kinesthetic gave him access to the feelings of exhilaration and well-being in a variety of contexts.

We have a muscle memory, as anyone knows who has gotten on a bicycle after not having ridden one for years. It may be difficult to set the pattern, but once learned, the pattern is fixed. The pattern is a sequence of muscle firings, and it is the sequence and the particular muscular tensions that accompany them that holds us in specific internal states. As an experiment, hold your right hand, palm down, and place your thumb in your mouth in such a way that you can pinch your left cheek between the thumb and forefinger. Move your thumb all the way back in your mouth, pinch your cheek, and give it several tugs forward and out. Notice the sensation in your cheek. What does it remind you of?

Do it again, only this time remember the sensations in the sequence of an injection of novocaine. This is an experience that is familiar to all of us and that has common elements. There are sensations of numbness, sometimes a slight tingling, a feeling of the tongue being swollen, of losing sensation in the lips. Trace the sequence of awareness carefully, feeling exactly what you felt the last time you had an experience with novocaine. Now repeat the sequence three or four times. Each time you repeat it, intensify the sensations. Notice what begins to happen. It is the kinesthetic memory at work. Each time you have an experience of novocaine your body experiences the same sequence. When you repeat that sequence, your body associates the sequence with the effects of the drug and you begin to re-experience novocaine. What will work with one drug will work with another.

EXERCISE: DRUG OF CHOICE

Singly.

Step 1. *Select a drug with which you are familiar. Select a drug, the effects of which you would like to duplicate without actually using the drug. A word of caution: do not select a drug that has unpleasant side effects—you will get them too.*

Step 2. *Remember some time when you had an experience with this drug. As you remember that experience, what was the first body sensation that let you know the drug was taking effect? Then the* *next. And the next. Trace the precise sequence of body sensations caused by the drug.*

Step 3. *Once you can identify the sensations and their sequence, begin to repeat the sequence, intensifying the sensations with each cycle.*

Most people think of this as a way to have fun, which it certainly can be, but Keith Hanson utilized the process in a slightly different way. His wife Sue was about to have their second child, and when she went into labor experienced rapid heartbeat, fluctuating blood pressure, extreme body tension that did not relax between contractions, and excruciatingly painful contractions. She could not be sedated because of the drug's effect on the baby. Keith had her re-experience morphine exactly as it is laid out in the exercise. Each time she ran the sequence, he anchored it—stacking anchors for the morphine experience. He then had her place the tips of her thumb and forefinger together and press. As she did that, he fired the anchor and transferred it to Sue's thumb and forefinger so that she could control it. He then set two other anchors the same way, utilizing the tips of her middle and ring fingers in combination with her thumb. The second anchor was the alpha/theta state between waking and sleep. The third anchor was a three-place dissociation, where she watched herself watch herself lying in the labor room. Since Sue was monitored for heartbeat and blood pressure, he had instant feedback. Within twenty minutes her blood pressure returned to normal, her heart rate returned to normal, and she knew when she was having a contraction because of the movement of her body. She remained comfortable throughout each contraction and relaxed immediately after it was over. She said she was sure she could have delivered the baby without anesthetic, but her first child had been a C-section and the doctor wanted to be prepared for immediate surgery if there were any complications. She was anesthetized and gave birth to a healthy baby boy.

You may have begun to notice that the point at which you become most aware of body sensation is not the place where the sensation originates. In other words, body sensations tend to flow: there is a direction to them. For the most part we tend to remain unaware of the movement of sensation, paying attention only to the more intense feelings at the place of arrival. It would be interesting to explore a possible correlation between the movement patterns of body sensation and the meridian lines used in acupuncture. Whether there is or is not a correlation between them, it is necessary to be able to sense the movement of body sensations in order to utilize kinesthetic sub-modalities effectively.

I began playing with the possibilities inherent in this and got myself quite happily drunk on one glass of wine. It was similar to the drug of choice exercise, but I had a glass of wine as a prop to signal each sequence. Later, it occurred to me to question what would happen if the process was reversed. In other words, find the movement of the sensations that accompany alcohol consumption and simply reverse the movement. The idea was too tempting to pass up and, maintaining the same social situation as with the wine, I drank more than half a fifth of Wild Turkey over a four-hour period and remained coherent, coordinated and precise in my diction. At 101 proof, that is enough alcohol to have left me fairly incoherent under ordinary circumstances. I have no idea what my blood-alcohol level would have been, but there was no unpleasant hangover the following morning. I mentioned it to the now grown-up Jessica who said, "Yeah, me and my girlfriend used to do that at parties. When the room would start to spin, we'd get it spinning the other way and be sober in fifteen minutes." So much for parental wisdom.

It had not occurred to me before this writing to explore the possibilities of utilizing this process to treat allergies. It does make sense. However, I did use the phenomenon of reversing the direction of body sensation as a way to control sleep. I made a marathon drive across country during which I was awake for forty hours. In the past, when I would get sleepy driving, I would open the windows, sing, slap my face, stop for coffee, or wash my face in cold water. None of it was particularly effective in keeping me awake. This time, I paid close attention to the body sensations that accompanied the 'I am getting sleepy' feeling. The sensation started in my face, around and behind my eyes. The sensation, a slight tingling, moved to the back of my head, down through my neck and shoulders, down through my chest and abdomen, to end in my lower abdomen. Once I became aware of that, it was relatively easy to move the sensation up and out. The result, a feeling of wakefulness, was almost instantaneous. There was one point on the trip where it did not work and the sensation was quite different. The feeling, which originated in my abdomen, was much more diffuse and spread throughout my body. I pulled over and slept for an hour and a half, awoke, feeling awake and refreshed and ready to continue the trip. Surprisingly, there was no crash at the end of the trip. I conducted a workshop and visited with friends over a five-day period and then repeated the same sequence on a return journey. The most interesting aspects were the differing sensations that accompanied my initial sleepiness as opposed to the real need to rest, the brevity of the rest necessary to rejuvenate and the continual sense of well-being.

Consider using the same procedure when someone is experiencing insomnia. One sub-modality approach to insomnia is to slow down the internal dialogue that accompanies the insomniac's attempts to sleep. The voice with which he speaks to himself can begin to slow down, to become quieter, less strident and begin to sound sleepy. That voice may even have to pause occasionally to yawn. Internal images can also be slowed down or dimmed to enhance sleep. There is also a kinesthetic component to insomnia. A person who cannot sleep may feel tired, but paradoxically he also feels wide awake. The feeling of being wide awake has accompanying body sensations. Trace the sensations of 'wide awake' from the point of origin to the point where they are most in awareness. Once the path of sensations has been mapped, reverse the direction. Couple the reversal of body sensations with a change in the internal dialogue to enjoy a full night's sleep.

Body sensations combined with system overlap can be utilized very effectively in trance induction. Recognizing the common kinesthetic elements of the trance state formed the basis of autogenic training: feelings of heaviness, warmth and movement. However, it is more effective to experience a trance state and to identify the sub-modality changes that take place.

EXERCISE: SUB-MODALITIES OF THE TRANCE STATE

In pairs.

Step 1. Person B paces A's breathing, speaking only on A's exhale. Pace his experience by telling him he is aware of three things that he can verify immediately. For example, "You can be aware of the weight of your body resting there on the chair." Then add the suggestion that "You can become very deeply relaxed."

Step 2. Repeat the sequence with two immediately verifiable comments and add, "And you can become even more deeply relaxed and comfortable."

Step 3. B asks A the following questions: (Do not pace breathing with question.)

As you sit there feeling relaxed and comfortable, what is it that you are aware of in your body? What else are you aware of?

B writes down A's complex equivalence for 'relaxed and comfortable.'

Step 4. B again begins to pace A's breathing and induces a trance state by making one more immediately verifiable sensory comment and adding a lead into the trance. For example, "As I speak to you, you can become aware of your breathing... of the flow of your breath... in... and out. And as you follow your breath... in... and out... you will be able to relax all the way into that trance state."

Step 5. B adds the suggestion, "While you remain comfortably in trance, you will be able to answer my questions."

Step 6. *B asks the following questions:*

On a scale of 1 – 10, with 1 as your relaxed state and 10 as the deepest trance you can imagine, how would you rate your present trance?

As you made the transition from the relaxed state to the trance state, what were you aware of in your body, what were the body sensations that let you know you were going into a trance?

And what was the next thing you were aware of?

> *Continue to trace the sequence of awareness, including internal visual and internal/external auditory awareness: A's complex equivalence for a trance state.*

Step 7. *When B has identified the patterns involved, ask A to reverse them. Take them one at a time, and repeat A's description and ask him to reverse that one, then go on to the next. Start with the last thing A became aware of and go back through the sequence to the beginning, that is, the first thing he was aware of.*

> *A will return to the relaxed state and open his eyes.*

Step 8. *Ask A to repeat the sequence of sub-modality changes that accompanied the induction of the trance state. This is the same as tracing the sequence of kinesthetic awareness you did in 'Drug of Choice.'*

Step 9. *B asks A to rate this trance on a scale of 1 – 10, as before. Check for additional sub-modality awareness in all systems.*

Step 10. *Repeat the process, reversing directions as appropriate. Ask A to intensify the sensations*

and speed the movement until he is able to shift in
and out of trance quickly and easily.

As you begin to recognize the difference in trance
ratings and the sub-modalities that accompany them,
you can predetermine the depth of trance you will
achieve. With a little practice, you can become quite
adept at changing the sub-modalities of the waking state
to those of the trance state. This is a very effective and
rapid self-induction technique. When working with
another person, you can anchor the induction sequence
with a hand gesture and one or two key phrases to
achieve a very rapid induction. When using the process
as a self-induction, it is helpful to deepen the trance in
stages, using the sub-modalities to return to a wakeful
state and then reversing them to go even deeper. Program
the self-induced trance at the beginning, when you are in
a relaxed, waking state: set a time frame and your
intention for the trance. (See *TRANCEFORMATIONS* by Bandler and Grinder for a detailed discussion of self-hypnosis
and process inductions.)

Not only do trance states have a kinesthetic component; every human response has its own unique kinesthetic coding, and the rhythmic pattern is a significant
part of that code. Rhythmic patterns are reflected in a
person's breathing pattern, gestures, walk, speech
rhythms and in their internal dialogue. The way people
are most aware of internal rhythms are the little
snatches of song they sing to themselves or hear inside
their heads. We also tap our fingers, pat our feet, nod our
heads. In fact, the body is in constant motion.

Stop for a minute or two and pay attention to your own internal rhythm in your present state of consciousness. If you have difficulty identifying your rhythms, begin to tap your fingers and allow the rhythm to develop. Another way to approach this is to pay attention to any internal dialogue that comes up and match the speech rhythm of that. Once you have identified the internal rhythm of your present state, remember some time when you were having fun, some time that was really fun and exciting. What happens to your internal rhythm as you change your state with that remembered fun and excitement? Play with this, noticing the rhythmic changes as you remember a time when you were sad, when you were angry, a time when you were frightened or when you were making love.

The next step in this is to discover that you can change the rhythm arbitrarily. That is, you can speed it up or slow it down in the same way that you can brighten or dim an internal image. Remember that time when you were having fun and begin to speed up the internal rhythm, then slow it down and notice how the feelings of the memory are more or less intense with each change. How does the speed of your rhythm effect the image? Explore the sub-modality trance induction once more, paying particular attention to the rhythmic changes that accompany the trance state. Notice whether this gives you more control and flexibility in changing consciousness.

Dennis O'Connor developed an exercise that gives you practice in changing internal rhythms and in calibrating to the subtle cues of another person's rhythmic patterns.

EXERCISE: RHYTHMIC CALIBRATION

Group of three, with A as subject, B as programmer and C as director. Stand in the following relationship to one another.

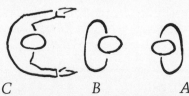

C   B   A

Step 1. *A identifies his internal rhythm and provides overt expression of that rhythm by nodding his head, tapping his foot, patting his thigh, etc., as a way of communicating the rhythm to B and C.*

Step 2. *C signals A to speed up or slow down while B calibrates to the external changes that accompany the rhythmic shifts. C needs to allow B time to calibrate before signaling another change.*

Step 3. *When B thinks she has calibrated to the rhythmic cues, she informs A, who stops the conscious overt expression of his rhythm.*

Step 4. *B then tells A a story, matching her voice rhythms to A's internal rhythm. C continues to signal faster or slower.*

If B fails to match the rhythmic changes, C signals A to again repeat the overt expression until B has a chance to re-calibrate.

When B has correctly paced six rhythmic changes, switch roles.

It's surprising how little practice it takes to be able to match another person's internal rhythm. You can also begin to notice that you can do this at a considerable distance. In workshops, I send people out to pace someone's rhythm in a restaurant, park, or other public place. The minimum distance is twenty feet. After pacing the other person, the workshop participants then change their own rhythms in such a way that they get a verifiable response from the person they have been pacing. The results are startling. We communicate on levels far out of our conscious awareness. You can use rhythmic matching as a way to gain group rapport in teaching, or for pace and lead patterns in one-on-one communication. When doing hypnosis, if you first pace the other person's internal rhythm and then begin to slow your own rhythm, the process is guaranteed to enhance any induction technique.

Chris Hall used what she called the Groovy Swish. This is essentially a collapse anchors utilizing internal rhythms keyed to music. The way it works is to think of some limitation you have, then begin to hear a piece of music inside your head that matches the way you feel. Then change the music. The music you are listening to now matches the way you would like to feel in that situation. It's helpful to have someone else cue the music change. The music rhythm is an anchor for the limitation, and the radical shift in music rhythm is a content-free counter-anchor. It's a nice, fun piece and so simple.

We have only begun to scratch the surface of the utilization of kinesthetic sub-modalities. Whatever the potential, kinesthetic sub-modality changes can be used to enhance sub-modality patterns in other systems. Whether you are using the swish pattern, utilizing sub-modalities for trance induction, or simply having a person change one set of sub-modalities for another, including body sensations provides a more powerful shift of his internal states. For some people with a strong kinesthetic, the visual swish is difficult. In these cases, use the kinesthetic as a way for them to access the visual portions of their experience. People will often describe an image without an auditory portion, but there is always a kinesthetic accompaniment that can be utilized to enhance their changes.

Appendix

Sometimes we respond to an event in the contemporary world in such a massive overreaction that it does not make sense. I worked with a woman in a workshop setting who had been asked to give a presentation to fellow workers about a project she had been engaged in. She is a competent person who had all of the necessary information to make the presentation. Not quite in the category of a speech, this was more an oral report on her project. What she said about the experience was that she had anticipated five or six people and was surprised when a dozen came to hear what she had to say. She was struck with stage fright and could barely talk. The only thing she was able to do was to read her notes, never taking her eyes off the page.

I was doing a demonstration of the swish pattern, which seemed appropriate. We began with a large picture of what she saw at the time and a little picture in the corner in which she saw herself responding in the situation the way she wanted to. Standard swish pattern technique. I was not satisfied with the way in which she responded, and I said, "Why don't you take over? I'm sure people have questions to ask about your experience." I walked out of the room and watched what happened. It was a little better than the earlier stage fright she had described, but not much. Why did the swish fail? Everything seemed appropriate, but there had to be a piece missing.

I came back into the room and began talking about old images that hang around and get triggered by things that happen in the present. These old memories have images that are so dark they are not seen, remaining out of consciousness, but that result in a response that does not make sense. We are not responding to what is happening in the present, rather to what happened in the past. It's almost a phobic response, and the memory remains out of consciousness. It is as if there were an image overlay—one picture on top of the other.

I continued to talk on about the possibilities of memory images that remained out of consciousness and the need to brighten that picture and bring it into focus so that the memory could be responded to directly. Suddenly she said, "I just remembered a time when I was three years old and there was a big party at my parents' house. Somebody put me up on a card table and I was supposed to sing. All the adults were standing around laughing and pointing at me. It was awful." Since we were demonstrating swish patterns, we swished the image of the adults laughing and pointing to an image in which she saw herself as the three-year-old responding in an appropriate way. Then we went back to the scene in her office and swished that the same way we had done it originally. She had a different response this time, and when I left the room she remained quite comfortable sitting in front of thirty-five people describing what had just happened and answering their questions.

Later she told us that when she had first attempted the swish, she had been unable to put faces on the group in her office presentation, and she could not put a head on herself having made the changes she wanted to. After working with the three-year-old memory, she was able to see faces on the people in her office and a head on herself responding the way she liked. She has since been happily teaching workshops in her area of expertise.

Some interference with the image memory of the experience a person is attempting to work with seems characteristic of the double image. In some instances, a person who has demonstrated the ability to make sub-modality changes in memory images is unable to change one particular memory. One of my clients, who is a skilled abstract painter, described an experience in which he brought several paintings to a photographer to have them photographed before sending them to a show. What bothered him was that it took him forty-five minutes before he could "get enough nerve" to tell the photographer that the paintings were upside down. As he said, it doesn't make sense. It doesn't make sense to the rational adult standing in the photographer's studio, but it does make sense somewhere. The image in the photographer's studio seemed fixed and he was unable to effect any sub-modality change. Since he had been able to use the swish pattern with other experiences quite successfully, it eliminates the issue of someone who has difficulty with visualization.

I began to talk about image overlays, old memories with images that are so dim they could not be seen and that distorted the images of recent events. This was much the same discussion as with the lady who had stage fright. He suddenly remembered an experience when, as a two-year-old, he had been locked in a closet as punishment. In this instance, the memory was indeed dim, but as he recalled the experience, he could see light coming under the door and through the cracks and could make out the vague outline of objects in the closet.

We used Robert Dilts' re-imprinting pattern with the two-year-old memory. When we returned to the experience in the photographer's studio, there was a spontaneous change in the brightness of the image and he was able to be quite flexible in making other sub-modality changes.

One possibility that would be a fruitful area for research is that the person who is experiencing depression is remembering through a screen of an old, out-of-consciousness image. One of the interesting things about people who are depressed is that they can have a good time, but when they think back on it, even a few hours later, they cannot remember the good-time feelings. Something gets in between them and their recent memory. There was a woman in a workshop who was laughing and joking with people before the lunch break. When she returned after lunch, she was asked if she had had a good time in the morning. She thought about it and said, "Well, you were having a good time." Although she was chronically depressed, she could still enjoy herself. What she could not do was remember the good time.

Some people experience spontaneous sub-modality changes in their perceptions of the outside world. I had a client who had a seven-year history of catatonic episodes. The first thing I wanted to know was how he got out. I did not want to be working with someone who disappeared inside with no way to get him back. He said, "I was in the hospital and I couldn't move. I was in a lot of pain because my neck was twisted way over on the side. Then this attendant started shooting rubber bands at me. I thought, I'm supposed to be sick and he's supposed to be healthy, and I got really pissed off and told him what I thought of him." I said, "You ought to buy the dude a box of cigars 'cause he got you mad enough to get you out. And before we go any further, I got a whole drawer full of rubber bands and if you don't come out when I tell you... zap, right in the kisser." So we had a joke and a good anchor.

The next question was how he got in. He said, "I kinda space out." What happened to him was that his visual field narrowed, darkened and went out of focus. Then he started to hallucinate onto the dark, fuzzy image. His world would become peopled with scary monsters. He looked weird when he did this because he would become immobile, with his mouth open and his eyes in a fixed stare. It would happen to him spontaneously in public, which frightened people like waitresses, who called the cops. What would happen then is that he experienced an attack by the scary monsters as the cop would shake him and ask what was wrong. That would frighten him so much he couldn't get out. Back to the hospital he would go.

I had him do it again, deliberately. He was good and it only took a minute or so before I became a scary monster. I told him to look around and find a knob, like on a TV set. This knob controlled the angle of view, brightness and focus. He nodded to indicate he had such a knob and I told him to turn it down even more, but not all the way to black. Then I told him to turn it the other way so that what he saw would broaden, get brighter and sharper in focus as he continued to turn the knob. Suddenly, he said, "Wow. I came out." I said, "Great, go back in."

We practiced for twenty minutes or so. He enjoyed it so much he decided to calibrate his knob and was able to exhibit some highly refined discriminations in the extent to which he altered his perceptions. Finally, I said, "Look, if it serves some useful purpose for you to go into this state, by all means go there. The important thing for me is that you are in control." I saw him again two weeks later and he related several instances where he had been able to bring himself back appropriately. A month later, he told me, "It's interesting, I don't have to do that any more."